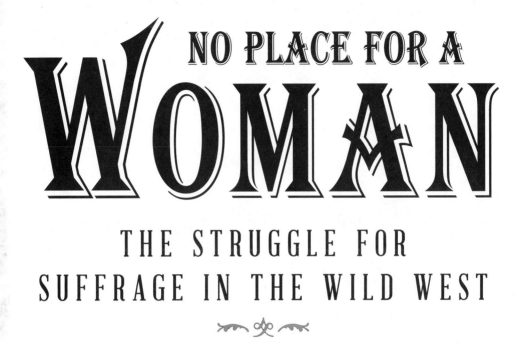

NO PLACE FOR A WOMAN

WOMAN

THE STRUGGLE FOR SUFFRAGE IN THE WILD WEST

CHRIS ENSS

WITH AN INTRODUCTION BY ERIN H. TURNER

TWODOT®

Helena, Montana
Guilford, Connecticut

A · TWODOT® · BOOK

An imprint and registered trademark of The Rowman & Littlefield Publishing Group, Inc.
4501 Forbes Blvd., Ste. 200
Lanham, MD 20706
www.rowman.com

Distributed by NATIONAL BOOK NETWORK

British Library Cataloguing in Publication Information available

Library of Congress Cataloging-in-Publication Data available

ISBN 978-1-4930-4891-5 (hardcover)
ISBN 978-1-4930-4892-2 (e-book)

♾™ The paper used in this publication meets the minimum requirements of American
National Standard for Information Sciences—Permanence of Paper for Printed Library
Materials, ANSI/NISO Z39.48-1992.

CONTENTS

———•◦•———

Failure is impossible. Library of Congress

ACKNOWLEDGMENTS

———•●•———

The idea of writing a book about the suffrage movement west of the Mississippi seemed a monumental undertaking. The inspiration needed to press forward came from social reformer and women's rights activist Susan B. Anthony. "Failure is impossible," Miss Anthony reminded those fighting for women's right to vote in 1906. It was with that in mind that the work could be completed.

In addition to thanking dedicated suffragists like Susan B. Anthony, the following organizations and individuals deserve recognition for their support and help in making this volume possible.

The ladies at the Nevada County Historical Society for compiling the correspondence between Mr. & Mrs. Sargent and Susan B. Anthony, including Senator Aaron Sargent's draft of what would eventually become the Nineteenth Amendment.

Utah State Historical Society

Oregon State Historical Society

U.S. National Park Service

Library of Congress

Coi Drummond-Gehrig at the Denver Public Library

Maria Shriver, author and former First Lady of California

John Priest, associate publicity manager at Rowman & Littlefield Publishing for never failing to do what's necessary to promote a title.

And to editor Erin Turner—without her this book would be woefully lacking. It is her dedication and drive that has seen this project through and made it a rewarding venture.

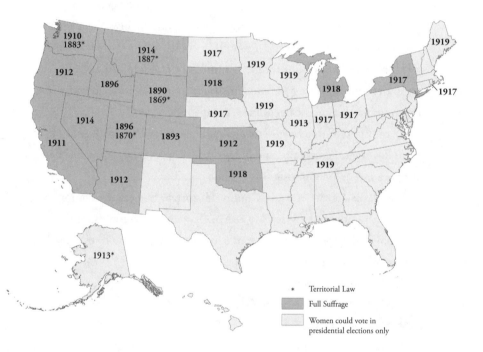

1910
1883*

1914
1887*

1917

1919

1919

1919

1912

1896

1890
1869*

1918

1918

1917

1914

1896
1870*

1893

1917

1919

1913

1917

1917

1911

1912

1918

1919

1917

1917

1919

1919

1913*

* Territorial Law

Full Suffrage

Women could vote in
presidential elections only

INTRODUCTION

WOMEN'S WORK

by Erin H. Turner

*Never doubt that a small group of thoughtful, committed citizens
can change the world; indeed, it's the only thing that ever has.*

—MARGARET MEAD

July 9, 1848, Waterloo, New York. It was a hot Sunday afternoon, and Jane Hunt, wife to prominent Quaker Richard P. Hunt, was home tending her two-week-old daughter and awaiting the arrival of the guests she expected for afternoon tea. Hunt's home, an elegant, federal-style mansion, was comfortable and well-appointed, though not overtly luxurious, as befit her Quaker faith. It was the perfect venue for a meeting between a group of local Quaker women and renowned speaker, minister, and champion of reform Lucretia Mott, who was in the area visiting from Philadelphia. Mott, a Quaker minister, had been speaking openly in public and advocating fiercely for the abolition of slavery since the 1830s.

Hunt likely looked forward to the tea party and to the lively discussion she expected with Mott; her friend and fellow Quaker Mary Ann McClintock; Mott's sister, Martha Wright; and an acquaintance of Mott's named Elizabeth Cady Stanton. Mary Ann McClintock was the wife of the local Quaker minister—both she and he were adherents to a branch of Quakerism called Hicksites, which promoted equality between the sexes. Martha Wright was well known for her intellect, her witty commentary, and for her support of her sister's work and beliefs. Elizabeth Cady Stanton, who had first met Mott when the two were excluded from participation in the 1840 World's Anti-Slavery Convention in London on the basis of their sex, was also in attendance as she was visiting from nearby Seneca Falls, New York. Stanton took the opportunity, while the women enjoyed tea and dainty treats in Hunt's spacious and comfortable parlor, to unleash "a torrent of [her] long-accumulating discontent," over the inequality of the sexes.

The women's decision to meet that afternoon was no whim. As part of a group of progressive Quakers who had been active in the abolition

Lucretia Mott. Library of Congress

movement, they were well versed in strategic and political tactics and supported by spouses and families with similar convictions. The Waterloo community held that not only were men and women equal in the sight of God, inspired by their own inner divine light, but that women and men should work and live in equality within marriage. They also promoted women's rights to hold religious meetings with men and to speak before mixed groups. Stanton, the only non-Quaker in attendance at Jane Hunt's tea party, recalled a vow that she and Mott had made to hold a meeting solely to discuss the rights of women—a response to their humiliating exclusion from the London abolition event. The group determined to finally schedule a woman's rights convention—with Lucretia Mott as the featured guest speaker. And in Jane Hunt's carpeted and wallpapered parlor, the women drafted an invitation to the Wesleyan Chapel at Seneca Falls, New York, for July 19 and 20. A notice immediately went into the *Seneca County Courier*, declaring their intention. They would meet two weeks later—the event would come to be known as the Seneca Falls Women's Rights Convention.

Mott, Stanton, Hunt, McClintock, and Wright were just a few women representative of a large and growing group of men and women who, in the decades prior to 1848, had begun agitating for changes in women's status in American life. In the first half of the nineteenth century, it was assumed that before marriage, a woman's father would dictate her role in society. He could send her out to work for wages and keep those wages. He could control who she married and when. Common law stated that women couldn't inherit property, serve on juries, sign contracts—and certainly could not vote in elections, though in recent years property laws had evolved in New England. After marriage, most women quickly learned that their husbands would similarly direct their lives and control their property and determine their fates.

An underlying principle behind the segregation of women's roles in the mid-nineteenth century was the notion that women were expected

We want our rights. Library of Congress

to live up to what is now known as the "Cult of True Womanhood." The "ideal" woman was—regardless of her family or economic circumstances—required to be pious, pure, domestic, and submissive. An underlying tenet of this belief was that women should be sequestered at home in order that they might be the guardians of the family and of morals unsullied by the wickedness in the larger world. The woman's sphere was the home—as any attempt to defy her sequestration might adversely affect her more delicate health and might contaminate her purity. Regardless of the theory, of course women continued, as they always had, to labor endlessly in the domestic sphere and as part of family economies on farms and in small businesses. Many also worked for wages outside the home in growing industries or in home-based cottage industries like sewing and laundry, but for considerably less compensation than their male counterparts. For some women, the restrictions chafed and they turned their moral authority toward pressing issues of the day; because of the relative ease of their lives in the increasingly industrial age and access to educational opportunities, they finally had time and leisure to do so.

During the period of religious reform known as "the Second Great Awakening," which began during the last decade of the eighteenth century and continued into the first decades of the nineteenth century, many women had come to take a larger role in leadership in newly established and evolving churches and in reform movements. In the 1840s, the progressive causes of temperance and abolition attracted the zeal of reforming women. Elizabeth Cady Stanton had given her first public speech, a talk on temperance peppered with a healthy dose of women's rights, to an audience of women in Seneca Falls, New York, in November 1841. Starting in 1846, women's groups began meeting publically in Philadelphia and Massachusetts, part of the growing groundswell of discontent with women's proscribed and restricted place, but with the stated intention of forwarding the issues of abolition and temperance. Their indignation toward the evil practice of slavery and the dangers of alcohol was fueled by the very cult that told them their sphere was the home and the protection of morality. But more and more women were conveniently putting aside the notion that their work had to be "at home."

The story of the early advocates for women's rights unfolds over familiar historical territory, following the narrative arch of America's story of promise and progress. Most states had, by the 1830s, granted suffrage to all white men regardless of their property-owning status. And men and women had begun to come together to fight against the institution of slavery, giving women political power that was previously unknown. By the late 1840s, when the abolitionist movement was still growing, America was firmly in the grip of the Victorian Age, but also on the precipice of massive change.

Two weeks after the tea and indignation at Jane Hunt's house, more than one hundred men and women would gather to declare, "We hold these truths to be self-evident, that all men *and women* are created equal,

Susan B. Anthony, circa 1900. Library of Congress

that they are endowed by their creator with certain inalienable rights, that among these are life, liberty, and the pursuit of happiness" at Seneca Falls, New York. It was a radical notion—and one that necessarily included the idea that woman should have the power of the vote.

With hindsight, the events of the ensuing decades seem inevitable. However, from the beginning of the women's rights movement, there were fissions due to the competing interests of abolition that threatened its progress. The supporters of both movements could fit neatly into

Elizabeth Cady Stanton. Library of Congress

the intersection of a Venn diagram, but needs for expediency necessarily drew support from one to the other. Still, some leaders questioned whether the support of woman's rights might set back those of the slaves they hoped to free. Additionally, groups that might ordinarily have supported suffrage were reluctant because of the tinge of temperance in the movement. And then the shots at Fort Sumter drew all of the momentum from the movement. During the Civil War years, the abolition of slavery and the support of Union troops took priority over the issues of women's rights and amendments to the Constitution. Then during Reconstruction when some suffrage advocates pushed for the inclusion of women in the Fifteenth Amendment, and failed, the women's rights movement split into two groups and two main organizations: the National Woman Suffrage Association (NWSA), which began to advocate for a universal suffrage amendment to the Constitution, and the American Woman Suffrage Association (AWSA), which wanted to take a state-by-state approach to achieving the vote. As a result of infighting and bitter fractures between old allies, it would be forty years before a more unified national approach would coalesce again around the franchise, and another ten years—and another war—before universal suffrage would be passed.

But while these events were unfolding in the East, a simultaneous wave of settlers was making its way west. The Civil War had largely derailed suffrage efforts, but not only did it not halt the westward progress of emigrants, it precipitated settlement in some areas, particularly immediately after the war as former soldiers from both sides of the conflict sought to start over. Starting in the 1830s, and reaching a peak between 1846 and the end of the Civil War, the Oregon Trail served as a pathway for nearly half a million emigrants who set off to the West to form new communities and societies from their individual stakes as farmers, settlers, ranchers, and miners. Most of the emigrants were men, and women rarely tackled the overland journey. Men could make the journey alone as drovers for

Woman Suffrage in the United States: A Timeline

1776	Abigail Adams writes to her husband, John Adams, asking him to "remember the ladies" in the new code of laws being discussed by the Continental Congress.
1777	Women formally lose the right to vote in New York.
1780	Women formally lose the right to vote in Massachusetts.
1784	Women formally lose the right to vote in New Hampshire.
1787	The Constitution grants the states the power to pass laws extending or limiting the vote to their citizens. Most states only allow white males who are citizens and who own property or pay taxes to vote. Women in all states except New Jersey lose the right to vote.
1790	The state of New Jersey grants the vote to "all free inhabitants," including women.
1792	During the period known as the Enlightenment, Mary Wollstonecraft publishes *Vindication of the Rights of Women* in England.
1807	Women lose the right to vote in New Jersey, the last state to formally revoke the right after the U.S. Constitution is ratified.
1792–1856	The vote is stripped from free black men who previously held it in many northern states, including New Jersey and Pennsylvania. At the same time, states began removing the property-ownership qualifications for white men, and by the mid-1820s most property ownership laws were dropped, though some states required voters to be taxpayers.
1830	As the abolition movement grows, more and more women join. All-women anti-slavery associations are formed, and women like Sarah and Angelina Grimke make appeals to Southern women to work against slavery.
1838	Kentucky passes the first statewide law granting a few women the vote—the new law allows women who are heads of households in rural areas to vote in tax and school board elections.
1840	At the World Anti-Slavery Convention in London, well-known abolitionists Lucretia Mott, Elizabeth Cady Stanton, and other women are barred from participating due to their sex.
1848	At the First Women's Rights Convention, organized by Mott, Stanton, and others and held in Seneca Falls, New York, equal suffrage is proposed by Elizabeth Cady Stanton. The suffrage proposal is adopted by the convention, along with a "Declaration of Rights and Sentiments" that declares women equal to men.

1850	The women's rights convention held in October in Worcester, Massachusetts, attracts more than a thousand participants from eleven states. This will become an annual event until 1861. Other states also begin to hold women's rights conventions.
1861–1865	Over the objections of Susan B. Anthony, Elizabeth Cady Stanton, and others, women put aside suffrage activities to help with the war effort.
1866	Susan B. Anthony and Elizabeth Cady Stanton form the American Equal Rights Association, intended to work toward suffrage for both women and African Americans as the Reconstruction era begins.
1867	Elizabeth Cady Stanton, Susan B. Anthony, and Lucy Stone address the New York State Constitutional Convention to ask that the revised constitution include woman suffrage. Their efforts are unsuccessful.
1868	When the U.S. Congress passes the Fourteenth Amendment to the Constitution and it is ratified by the states, it is interpreted by many as excluding women from citizenship and the vote. The rift between former abolitionist allies and suffragists grows. However, in New Jersey, 172 women attempt to vote as a challenge to the Fourteenth Amendment's exclusionary language and are ignored.
1869	Frederick Douglass and other advocates of suffrage for black males, who were formerly allies of the woman suffrage movement, distance themselves from the fight for women's votes as the push to ratify the Fifteenth Amendment intensifies. The suffrage movement splits, and two groups are formed: The NWSA, under Elizabeth Cady Stanton as president, and the AWSA, with Julia Ward Howe as president. Anthony and Stanton make the controversial decision to ally themselves with former anti-abolitionist women in the South. Wyoming Territory grants women full suffrage as part of their new territorial constitution.
1870	The Fifteenth Amendment to the Constitution is ratified, providing that all men, regardless of "race, color or previous condition of servitude" have the right to vote, leaving it to the states to decide on the woman suffrage question. Stanton and Anthony oppose the amendment for neglecting the women; Lucy Stone and other former abolitionists support the amendment as a positive step for the formerly enslaved. More than forty women in Massachusetts attempt to vote. They cast their ballots but they are ignored. Utah Territory grants woman suffrage.
1871	The Anti-Suffrage Society is formed by men and women who actively campaign against woman suffrage. Victoria Woodhull, who will be the first woman to run for president in 1872, argues before the Judiciary Committee of the U.S. House of Representatives that women have the right to vote under the Fourteenth Amendment.

1872	Susan B. Anthony and her supporters register to vote in Rochester, New York, and are arrested at the polls. Anthony is arrested and is held on $1000 bail. Her sisters and eleven other women are also held on $500 bail. In the Dakota Territory, a suffrage bill before the legislature loses by just one vote. Victoria Woodhull is nominated to run for president of the United States by the Equal Rights Party.
1873	Anthony is denied a trial by jury when she fights her arrest. She's fined $100 plus costs, however she never pays the fine. A suffrage demonstration is held at the Centennial of the Boston Tea Party.
1874	Suffragists protest in favor of the vote at a centennial commemoration of the Battle of Lexington. The U.S. Supreme Court rules that being a citizen of the United States does not guarantee the right to vote and thus the Fourteenth Amendment does not guarantee woman suffrage. A referendum on woman suffrage in Michigan fails to pass. The Woman's Christian Temperance Union is formed.
1875	In Michigan and Minnesota, women win the right to vote in school elections.
1876	During centennial celebrations in Philadelphia on July 4, Susan B. Anthony reads "The Declaration for the Rights of Women" in front of a crowd gathered at the Liberty Bell.
1878	A federal woman suffrage amendment is introduced in the U.S. Congress by Senator A. A. Sargent of California, where it fails to pass.
1880	Lucretia Mott dies. New York State grants women the right to vote in school elections.
1882	Both chambers of the U.S. Congress appoint committees to study woman suffrage—the recommendation is for suffrage, though the lack of forward progress on the issue on the national scene belies the committees' efforts.
1883	Women in Washington Territory are granted full suffrage, though the territorial Supreme Court will overturn the law four years later.
1884	Belva Lockwood, the first woman attorney granted the privilege to argue before the Supreme Court, runs for president. Suffrage is debated in the U.S. House of Representatives.
1886	Suffragists and other women protest their exclusion from the dedication ceremonies for the Statue of Liberty. The suffrage amendment is voted on and defeated two to one in the U.S. Senate.
1887	Congress passes the Edmunds-Tucker Anti-Polygamy Act, which strikes down Utah Territory's woman suffrage measures. Kansas women win the right to vote in municipal elections. Rhode Island is the first eastern state to vote on a woman suffrage referendum, however, it does not pass. The Dawes Act technically makes Native American men who willingly disassociate themselves from their tribes eligible to vote.

1890	Wyoming is admitted to the union as a state; its woman suffrage provisions, in place since 1869, are not overturned as part of their admission. Nearly thirty years after their split, the NWSA and the AWSA merge to form the National American Woman Suffrage Association (NAWSA) and turn their attention toward a state-by-state approach to suffrage laws, working with the locally formed organizations. Elizabeth Cady Stanton is chosen as their first president. A campaign for full suffrage loses in South Dakota.
1893	After a vigorous campaign led by Carrie Chapman Catt from the national organizations and women like Ellis Meredith who organized statewide efforts, Colorado men vote for woman suffrage in the so-called Centennial State.
1894	Six hundred thousand signatures are collected on a petition in favor of woman suffrage in New York, but it fails to advance a bill in the legislature. Lucy Stone dies.
1895	Elizabeth Cady Stanton publishes her controversial *The Woman's Bible, a Critique of Christianity*, which causes her ouster from the NAWSA. The New York State Association Opposed to Woman Suffrage is formed.
1896	Idaho votes for woman suffrage. Ida Husted Harper is hired by the NAWSA to run a suffrage campaign in California—which fails.
1897	When Utah becomes a state, woman suffrage is included in its constitution, restoring the right first given to women in the territory in 1870. Publication of the NAWSA's *National Suffrage Bulletin*, edited by Carrie Chapman Catt, begins.
1900	Carrie Chapman Catt takes over the leadership of the NAWSA.
1902	Elizabeth Cady Stanton dies. Women from ten different countries, including the famous Civil War nurse Clara Barton, meet in Washington, D.C., to discuss international efforts toward suffrage. New Hampshire's male voters defeat a suffrage referendum.
1904	NAWSA adopts their declaration of principles, and Rev. Dr. Anna Howard Shaw becomes president of the organization when Carrie Chapman Catt resigns to care for her ailing husband.
1906	Susan B. Anthony dies. Harriot Stanton Blatch, daughter of Elizabeth Cady Stanton, forms the Equality League of Self Supporting Women, which aims to organize women professionals and workers in favor of the vote.
1907	The Equality League of Self Supporting Women begins following the lead of English suffragists who have been holding parades, speaking on streets, and picketing.
1910	Washington State grants women the right to vote after a decades' long grassroots campaign by many women, including Emma Smith DeVoe.

1911	California grants women suffrage. Harriot Stanton Blatch's Women's Political Union, the new name of the former Equality League of Self-Supporting Women, organizes a three thousand-person parade in New York City in support of the vote.
1912	Oregon grants women the right to vote, largely due to the untiring efforts of Abigail Scott Duniway, who split from the national AWSA in her locally focused bid to pass legislation in Oregon. Theodore Roosevelt's Progressive Party supports woman suffrage as part of their platform.
1913	Alice Paul's Congressional Union for Woman Suffrage (CU), born from the Congressional Committee of the NAWSA, tries to reinvigorate the national suffrage amendment, first introduced in 1878, by targeting Democratic candidates as being weak on women's suffrage. The CU is effective in getting an amendment introduced in the Senate for the first time in decades, however it fails, and their radical tactics alienate the other leaders of the NAWSA. Alaska Territory grants suffrage to female citizens. Illinois gives women municipal and presidential voting rights. The Southern States Suffrage Conference is held, and suffragists there begin work on strategies for state laws to enfranchise white women.
1914	Nevada and Montana both grant women universal suffrage after hard-fought grassroots campaigns in both states.
1915	Carrie Chapman Catt steps back in as the president of the NAWSA. There has been turmoil on the board under Anna Howard Shaw, who doesn't have the administrative expertise needed for the job.
1916	Alice Paul leads a group of women to break away from the NAWSA, forming the National Woman's Party. Woodrow Wilson promises that the Democratic Party platform will include an endorsement of woman's suffrage. Jeannette Rankin is elected to the House of Representatives by the State of Montana. She is the first woman elected to serve in the U.S. Congress.
1917	Beginning in January, the National Women's Party stages silent protests, posting "Sentinels of Liberty" at the White House. Starting in June, nearly five hundred women are arrested, and 168 are jailed. In November of that year, at the Occoquan Workhouse in Virginia, suffragists are beaten and abused by their jailers. Meanwhile, America enters World War I, and the NAWSA aligns with the war effort in a bid for support for the cause. Five states grant women presidential suffrage, but not full suffrage: North Dakota, Indiana, Nebraska, Rhode Island, and Michigan. Arkansas gives women the right to vote in primaries. New York, South Dakota, and Oklahoma grant women full suffrage, making New York the first eastern state to fully offer the franchise to women.

1918	After Representative Jeannette Rankin opens the debate, the suffrage amendment finally passes in the U.S. House with a two-thirds majority, forty years after its first introduction. The measure fails in the Senate, but President Wilson addresses the Senate giving his support for woman's suffrage for the first time and suffragists who have been jailed are released from prison and an appellate court rules that the arrests were illegal.
1919	Three states, Michigan, Oklahoma, and South Dakota, grant women full suffrage. On the national stage, the National Women's Party lights a "Watchfire for Freedom," a torch that is intended to stay lit until the U.S. Senate passes the suffrage amendment. After the Senate passes the amendment, the NAWSA meets at its annual convention in St. Louis, and Carrie Chapman Catt proposes transforming the association into the League of Women Voters.
1920	The Nineteenth Amendment, which has also been called the Susan B. Anthony Amendment, is ratified by Tennessee on August 18 and becomes law on August 26. The amendment states, "The right of citizens of the United States to vote shall not be denied or abridged by the United States or by any State on account of sex." Women are guaranteed the right to vote—though voting restrictions that apply to nonwhites still restrict voting for many American women.
1924	The Indian Citizenship Act is passed, granting citizenship and, theoretically, voting rights to Native Americans. Unfortunately, laws are still in place that limit voting in some segments of the population—including Native Americans.
1943	The Magnuson Act is passed, which gives Chinese immigrants the rights to citizenship and voting.
1952	The McCarran-Walter repeals restrictions to citizenship based on race that have been in place since the 1790 Naturalization Law. First-generation Japanese Americans gain citizenship and voting rights.
1964–1966	The Twenty-Fourth Amendment, which abolishes the poll taxes and literacy tests that were commonly used to limit voter access, is ratified by two-thirds of the states. Further restrictions on voting are removed through the passage of the Voting Rights Act of 1965 and the Supreme Court prohibits tax payments and wealth requirements as voting requirements.
1971	The voting age is lowered to eighteen when the Twenty-Sixth Amendment is ratified.
1984	Mississippi ratifies the Nineteenth Amendment, the last state to do so.

the large wagon trains or with a plan to mine, strike it rich, and return to their homes in the East.

But women were part of that wave of emigration and not as mere passengers on the overland trails. Women traveled west as part of families and on their own to seek new opportunities. The experience of crossing the plains changed many of them—and helped demonstrate their grit, even as they held onto their identities as the protectors of family and morality. In their new homes, women took on public roles due to economic necessity and the needs of the community. They earned more authority, and combined with their perceived moral directive, they began to influence politics individually and pragmatically. Women, all over the country, had taken on new roles during the war years while men were on the battlefield and after the war as they supported the families of those killed or maimed. Many of these women also headed west, including educated women who wanted professions but had hit societal roadblocks in their efforts to do so in the East. These pioneers carried their eastern values with them, but did not abandon the dissatisfactions they also held. Settlers across the West did not abandon either the zeal for reform or the notion that the gentle, pious presence of women would help "civilize" the West. If their new lives required pioneer women to forsake some of that gentleness in the face of hardship, they were often also able to seize more responsibility and power for the sake of survival.

By the 1870s, women in the West did have a different degree and kind of power than their eastern counterparts—and in Utah and Wyoming they even had the right to vote. And while the frontier was influenced by the ravages of war, the distance suffragists there had from the conflicts and infighting of the previous twenty years offered a fresh start.

As territorial governments formed in Montana, Colorado, and Wyoming, women settlers in the region lobbied their male representatives to "remember the ladies" in the new territorial constitutions, taking a page from Abigail Adams's famous exhortation to her husband, John, during

Women and children made up a significant part of the emigration movement of the nineteenth century. Library of Congress

the days of the Continental Congress. And some men listened. Their reasons for doing so were varied, from the idea that notoriety would bring publicity and more women settlers to the area to the idea that these gentle creatures would bring order and civilization. And there were those who assumed that women would vote as their husbands instructed, making a political calculation based on a numbers game.

Opposition to woman suffrage ran a wide gamut as well, from men who were concerned that giving women the right to vote would bring about the prohibition of alcohol, to those who simply believed that voting would damage women's health, to those who argued that women didn't need to vote when they had a male protector to do it for them.

In Wyoming, in 1869, the town of South Pass City had grown to a population of t from its beginnings as a stagecoach and telegraph station set up in the 1850s to support the stream of emigrants who were making their way west on the Oregon Trail, passing over the Sweetwater River and climbing South Pass before making their way to the Pacific Northwest. When gold was discovered in the area, miners and merchants came together in a classic "boom" that—along with the relative ease of traveling west that came with the completion of the transcontinental railroad—helped it become a thriving city by the time the Wyoming Territorial Legislature was formed.

Esther Hobart Morris arrived in the settlement that year and began a campaign to include woman's suffrage in the territorial constitution. As the story went, she invited both of the candidates for the territorial legislature to her home for a tea party designed to win them over to her cause. William H. Bright, the saloon owner who would win election as representative, would go on to introduce a woman's suffrage clause in the territorial constitution, possibly at the urging of Morris. When John A. Campbell, the territorial governor, signed the document in December of 1869, Wyoming's male voters had granted women over the age of twenty-one the right to vote. It would be widely reported to later generations that Esther Hobart Morris had hosted a very important tea party at her home in order to influence the outcome of the first territorial elections for women. And on September 6, 1870, a grandmother named Louisa Ann Swain stepped up to a ballet box in Laramie, Wyoming, and exercised that right, ushering in the era of western states' early foray into suffrage equality. It had been more than twenty years after Elizabeth Cady Stanton and Susan B. Anthony made their declaration of the rights of woman at Seneca Falls, New York, that the men of the Wyoming Territorial Legislature became the first voting body in the United States to grant women over the age of twenty-one the right to vote in general elections.

The movement in the West spread—much more quickly than it had done in the East. Overland pioneers like Abigail Scott Duniway, who was one of the leaders of the suffrage movement in Oregon, quickly became part of the movement to extend votes for women in the region.

Women also protested to gain the right to vote in Colorado. Suffragists established the Colorado Non-Partisan Equal Suffrage Association and approached women's organizations, churches, political parties, and charity groups to gain allies for their cause. And after agitating nonstop from 1877 on, the Women's Suffrage Referendum passed on November 7, 1893. The following year, Colorado became the first state to have elected female legislators.

Martha Hughes Cannon, the first woman elected to the Utah state senate—in 1896—was a polygamist wife, a practicing physician, and an astute and pioneering politician. Her husband was the Republican candidate; she, a Democrat, defeated him in that historic election. And in 1916, four years before she would be legally allowed to vote in an election, Montana's Jeannette Rankin was sent to Washington, D.C., as a member of the U.S. House of Representatives from Montana. Four years later, in 1920, Nellie Taloe Ross would be elected governor of Wyoming.

The fight for woman suffrage in the West wasn't a new, separate movement, distinct from the efforts in the East. But the fight proceeded with a sense of inevitability in the newly minted territories. The ideologies and reforming zeal that spread from the Great Awakening, to the fiery rhetoric of the abolitionist movement, to the emerging natural ally of the woman's movement—the temperance movement—weren't abandoned in the West. But those ideologies were tempered by circumstance and taken up by women who were part of the Cult of True Womanhood, but who had earned their reputation for Grit on the overland trails and as part of the new frontier. The women who agitated for their rights were sure of their worth—and aware of their power in the new communities springing up around gold strikes and homestead stakes. And they used the tools at their disposal to influence the outcome. They knew that their power came from the fact that they were women, not in spite of it.

Entitled "Representative Women," this lithograph, circa 1870, showcases the early leaders of the suffrage movement: (clockwise from top) Lucretia Mott, Elizabeth Cady Stanton, Mary Livermore, Lydia Maria Child, Susan B. Anthony, Grace Greenwood. Center: Anna Elizabeth Dickinson. Library of Congress

Susan B. Anthony
1820-1906

Born on February 15, 1820, Susan B. Anthony began her work for women's rights and the abolition of slavery before the Civil War. A native of Massachusetts, as an adult Anthony lived in Rochester, New York, where she became acquainted with the most famous abolitionists of the day, including William Lloyd Garrison, Wendell Philips, and Frederick Douglass. But it was her long friendship with Elizabeth Cady Stanton that helped galvanize her fight for the vote throughout her long life.

When Anthony was rejected as a speaker at a temperance meeting in Albany in 1852, she formed the Woman's New York State Temperance Society and Stanton became its president. The formation of the new organization led to a lifetime of campaigning for Anthony, who traveled the United States speaking in favor of her goals for the rest of her life.

Though her zealous pursuit of her work frequently brought criticism, especially in the years after the Civil War when the suffrage movement was plagued by division, by the 1890s, Anthony was hailed as a national hero. She finally retired in 1900 at the age of 80, passing on the leadership of the National American Woman Suffrage Association to Carrie Chapman Catt. Anthony died fourteen years before the ratification of the Nineteenth Amendment, in 1906.

Carrie Chapman Catt
1859-1947

Carrie Chapman Catt was the founder of the League of Women Voters and one of the instrumental women leaders who got American women the right to vote in 1920—with the help of some two million members of the NAWSA and many others who cared about expanding democratic rights to women in the United States.

Born in Wisconsin in 1854 and raised in Iowa, she was a schoolteacher and superintendent after graduating from Iowa State College. By the late 1800s, the Women's Suffrage Movement, where she worked as a field organizer with Susan B. Anthony, was her full-time cause.

Catt reorganized the NAWSA when she moved to New York in 1915. With her leadership and the enormous efforts of two million women who joined the association, the Women's Right to Vote Constitutional Amendment was passed by both Houses of Congress and ratified by thirty-two states in August 1920.

Once the vote was won, the purpose of the NAWSA was complete, and the organization was formally dissolved in 1925.

Catt proposed the establishment of a League of Women Voters at the 1919 association convention as an organization to bring together independent women who cared about society and the vital issues of the day, but who were nonpartisan in their study and advocacy of these issues.

Lucretia Coffin Mott
1793–1880

Born at the end of the eighteenth century as the principles of the U.S. Constitution were being shaped, Lucretia Coffin grew up a Quaker in Boston, encouraged by her father to study the principles of democracy. At age thirteen she was sent to a boarding school near Poughkeepsie, New York, she would later teach and become awakened to issues of women's rights. Due to her sex, she was paid only half the salary male teachers were receiving.

In 1811 she married James Mott, a fellow teacher from the school, and the couple moved to Philadelphia, where in about 1818, she became a minister in the Friends church. Throughout the 1820s, she traveled the country to speak on the topics of social reform, including temperance, the abolition of slavery, and peace.

In 1833 Mott attended the founding convention of the American Anti-Slavery Society, and then became president of the Philadelphia Female Anti-Slavery Society. Although her support of abolition met opposition within her Quaker congregation, she persisted in her work, founding the the Anti-Slavery Convention of American Women in 1837. After she and Elizabeth Cady Stanton were barred from participating in the World's Anti-Slavery Convention in London in 1848 because of their sex, the two women took up the cause of women's rights. From that time on, Mott's focus was firmly on the women's rights movement, even as she continued to advocate for abolition and the rights of freedmen.

Alice Paul
1886–1977

Single-minded is the adjective most used to describe Alice Paul, who devoted her life to gaining voting rights, and then equal rights, for women.

As a suffragist she succeeded when, in 1920, the Nineteenth Amendment to the United States Constitution gave women voting rights. But she did not live to see the Equal Rights Amendment pass, though she authored it in 1923 and then worked for fifty-four years to have it passed.

Paul attended Swarthmore College and the University of Pennsylvania, earning a bachelor's degree in biology, a master's in sociology, and a doctorate in economics. She went on to earn three law degrees, which gave her the tools to write the Equal Rights Amendment well and equip herself to debate its merits in legal circles.

Abigail Scott Duniway
1834–1915

Abigail Scott Duniway is recognized as the "mother of equal suffrage in Oregon." She was born in Illinois on October 22, 1834.

The Scott family moved to Oregon in 1852 and Abigail taught school at Polk County Village. It was there she met her husband, Ben C. Duniway, a young farmer and stockman in Clackamas County. In the early 1860s, an accident befell Mr. Duniway and it was necessary to move from the farm. Mrs. Duniway returned to teaching. After three years the family relocated to Albany. Abigail taught school there for a year then opened a millinery store there.

It was in 1859 that Mrs. Duniway first came into prominence through the publication of a book entitled *Captain Gray's Company or Crossing the Plains and Living in Oregon.* In the spring of 1871, she moved to Portland, bought a printing office, and started a weekly publication, *The New Northwest*, which at once attracted many readers.

Early on she espoused the doctrine of equal suffrage, and her advocacy of political rights for women met with unexpected favor in Oregon, Washington, and Idaho. Her address before the Constitutional Convention at Boise, Idaho, July 16, 1889, was a notable effort. Her talk resulted in securing a pledge from state officials and businessmen of Idaho to submit the question of equal suffrage to a vote at the first election following the territory's admission to statehood.

Upon the occasion of the celebration of Oregon's fortieth year of admission to statehood, held in the House of Representatives in Salem, February 14, 1899, when the joint assembly of the legislature and a large audience gathered, Mrs. Duniway was given the valedictory, or place of honor on the program.

One of the greatest speeches on the progress of all women toward equal political rights was made at the unveiling of the statue of Sacajawea at the Lewis and Clark Exposition in the summer of 1905. This was followed by the extending of an invitation to her by the late H. W. Goode, president of the exposition, to accept the date of October 6 as Abigail Scott Duniway Day at the fair. This was the first reception of its kind ever tendered to any woman, aside from royalty, by the official head of any international exposition.

In early January 1910, Mrs. Duniway was made a duly accredited delegate by Oregon's Governor Benson in Washington, D.C. There she made a strong plea for equal political rights and was accorded much consideration by distinguished men in attendance.

Elizabeth Cady Stanton
1815–1902

Elizabeth Cady Stanton, who signed the first call for a woman's rights convention in the United States, was born in Johnstown, New York, on November 12, 1815. She was the daughter of Judge Daniel Cady and Margaret Livingston Cady, both persons of exceptional educational refinement. As a child Elizabeth displayed unusual intelligence and began her education at Johnstown Academy. After finishing the coursework at her homeschool, she went to Mrs. Emma Willard's seminary in Troy, New York, where she was graduated in 1822.

In 1839 she met Henry Brewster Stanton, an anti-slavery orator of some note, and in 1840 they were married. Immediately after their wedding they went to London where the international anti-slavery convention was to be held.

Mrs. Stanton was one of the delegates from America but was denied participation in the proceedings because she was a woman. While in London she met Lucretia Mott and with her signed the first call for a women's rights convention. Returning to Boston, Mr. and Mrs. Stanton made their home there until Mr. Stanton was compelled to move to Seneca Falls, New York, because of his health. It was in Seneca Falls on the 19 and 20 of July 1848, in the Wesleyan chapel, that the first women's rights convention was held. Mrs. Stanton was at the head of the movement at that time and, besides caring for the delegates, wrote the Declaration of Rights and Sentiments which became the subject of ridicule and jest throughout the United States.

From 1867 to 1874 she went from state to state campaigning for woman's suffrage and became associated with numerous organizations having that end in view. She became a candidate for Congress from the Eighth New York District, having the support of the *New York Herald*. She became associated in the management of the resolution with Susan B. Anthony and was the joint author of many books on woman's suffrage.

Lucy Stone
1818–1893

Born in Massachusetts in 1818 and educated at Oberlin College, Lucy Stone lectured widely against slavery and, on behalf of women's suffrage, helped organize the first national women's rights convention and the American Woman Suffrage Association and published the influential *Woman's Journal*.

After graduating from Oberlin College in 1847, Stone became a lecturer for the Massachusetts Anti-Slavery SocietyThrough her work on abolition, Stone became convinced the legal positions of women and slaves were not dissimilar. As her views developed, Stone spent part of her time speaking about women's issues, and in1850 she organized the first national Women's Rights Convention in Worcester, Massachusetts.

In 1855 Stone married Henry B. Blackwell, a fellow abolitionist. At their wedding the couple read and signed a document that protested the legal rights that were traditionally given to a husband over his wife. The word "obey" was pointedly removed from the marriage vows and instead, the two promised to treat each other equally. Stone also announced that would henceforth be addressed as Mrs. Stone. This action drew national attention, and women who retained their maiden names were soon known as "Lucy Stoners."

After the Civil War, Stone and Blackwell shifted their focus from abolition to women's suffrage. In 1869 Stone helped form the AWSA, which worked for women's suffrage on a state by state basis, seeking amendments to state constitutions. Stanton and Anthony established a rival organization, the NWSA, which sought an amendment to the U.S. Constitution.

Stone edited the *Woman's Journal*, a weekly suffrage journal, for many years, eventually turning the task over to her daughter, Alice Stone Blackwell

When the AWSA and the NWSA merged into the NAWSA in 1890, Stone became the chair of the executive committee.

Chapter One

***

Esther Hobart Morris and Woman Suffrage in Wyoming

Never let the truth stand in the way of a good story, unless you can't think of anything better.

—Mark Twain

Esther Hobart Morris carefully arranged borrowed chairs and warmed, borrowed teacups as she prepared for her visitors to arrive. Her tiny mountain cabin, perched at seventy-five hundred feet of elevation in the mountains at South Pass City, Wyoming Territory, was cleaned, decorated, and full of all of the delectable morsels she could contrive for the important guests who would be arriving soon. Her husband, John Morris, was barely tolerant of the bustle as he nursed a foot swollen with gout, but he didn't make his objections audible. The couple had only been in South Pass City a few months, and the time had not been easy for him, though Esther had leapt into local life with her usual enthusiasm. Her son from her first marriage, Archibald Slack, was soon to arrive to report on the afternoon's event for the newspaper. His story would appear in time for the elections that were to be held the next day in the boomtown of two thousand men, women, and children. White men would be voting to send delegates to Wyoming's Territorial Convention.

*Esther Hobart Morris was a staunch supporter of
the vote and the first woman to serve as Justice of
the Peace in the United States.* Library of Congress

Everything about the scene Esther set that day in her tiny home was
right by her standards and the standards of the day. The room was cozily
domestic, and any Victorian in 1869 would have felt at ease with the
ritual that was about to take place. The pouring of tea by a proper wife
and mother, the gathering of friends over small plates of sandwiches
and desserts, removed gently from cherished china with delicate tongs,
the feathers and frills worn by the women and the ridges from hats just
removed remaining in the hair of the gentlemen were both comforting
and comfortable. But the gentle talk of community events and shared
acquaintance of an elegant tea would give way to the talk that was dominating South Pass City on that fall day—the territorial elections of the
next day and the future of Wyoming Territory itself. And that was exactly
what Esther Morris intended.

Americans love a good story of triumph over adversity—particularly the stories of our pioneering forbearers who set out to forge a new world for themselves on the frontier. The story of Esther Hobart Morris fits that profile perfectly. It is easy to imagine her on that fateful day, with the lines on her curl-framed face that mapped a life full of pioneering adventure and tragedies survived. Her clear-eyed gaze would have reflected the iron spine forged by years of hardship and striving toward her ideals—and a life of determination. Hers was a narrative of iconic, dramatic moments. It matched the story of Manifest Destiny, tracing the fate of a nation from ocean shore to ocean shore over the centuries, an inevitable march toward progress, punctuated with dramatic events and the iconic moments that reveal a story in a few words that stir political pride and bring to life a heroic pose in history: the famed Boston Tea Party, a people using the national beverage of its founding people to make a point. The Tea Party held by Jane Hunt in Waterloo, New York, where Elizabeth Cady Stanton and Lucretia Mott formed the plans for the 1848 Women's Rights Convention in Seneca Falls, New York. And the Tea Party where Esther Hobart Morris took on the idea of Women's Suffrage for the new Territory of Wyoming in 1869.

On the guest list for the event that afternoon was William Bright, who was standing for election as a Democrat. On the menu were tea cakes and talk of rebellion—could Wyoming be the very first territory to not just advocate for but legalize equal rights for women? Changes were on the horizon for the new territory, which needed to grow if it had hope of statehood. And in the boom-and-bust economy, there were six men to every woman in the territory. Men were thinking about what it might mean to publicity for the state and to attracting more women to settle there. And as more educated and politically minded women had made their way into the West, their advocacy had grown.

The problem with the Esther Hobart Morris tea-party story is that it's apocryphal at best, but it succeeds as a parable for the suffrage movement in the West and the direction it took after Wyoming opened the floodgates. Morris's contribution to achieving women's suffrage in Wyoming cannot be denied, however. The tale of her efforts to put her chosen candidate in office doesn't begin to reveal the whole story of woman's suffrage in Wyoming—the territory that would claim honors as the first to grant women the right to vote and the state that would be first to have a woman governor.

Morris fills an important role in the story of progress in the West. She exemplified the independent woman pioneer. She was born in Tioga County, New York, on August 8, 1814, and was orphaned at a young age. She had become a successful businesswoman by her early twenties, running a millinery business from her grandparents' home, and starting in the early 1830s, she was an outspoken opponent of slavery and an active proponent of women's rights. She married Artemus Slack in 1841, and when she was widowed in 1845, she learned firsthand how difficult it was for women to handle legal matters, particularly regarding property ownership when she moved to Illinois to handle her late husband's property. She was living in Peru, Illinois, in 1850, when she married local merchant John Morris. Eighteen years later, they would head west to the boom town of South Pass City, Wyoming Territory, settling there in the spring of 1868.

Suffrage efforts in the East had largely stalled in the late 1860s, because of the disruption of the Civil War, continuing male attitudes about women's proper role, and infighting in the suffrage movement itself. But in Wyoming, men could see that women were not only successful at protecting the hearth and home, they were also working side by side with men in businesses and community building. In political circles, discussions were beginning about the many reasons the Wyoming Territory might want to extend voting rights to the women in the territory—including attracting more women to a region where adult males outnumbered females six to one. Opponents to suffrage had an arsenal of excuses to hand. The postwar need for recovery and for men to regain

Abolitionists and Suffragists

The movement for woman suffrage, which began in 1846, was for a time overshadowed by the abolition movement. Virtually all women's rights advocates supported abolition, but not all abolitionists supported woman suffrage. Numerous abolitionists believed it was inappropriate for women to engage in public political actions. Feeling that their servitude was more deplorable than the political, legal, and economic disabilities of the women of the United States, many women suffragists gave their time, energy, and money to the freeing of African Americans.

When the Civil War had ended, and the Fourteenth Amendment was under discussion, Susan B. Anthony, Elizabeth Cady Stanton, and other leaders learned with amazement and indignation that it was proposed to put the word "male" in the Constitution of the United States, which before that time had not discriminated against women. The suffragists immediately petitioned Congress. When the Thirteenth Amendment abolishing slavery was pending, the women had been encouraged by both Republicans and abolitionists to send petitions to Congress. They collected more than three hundred thousand names. Several Republican senators applauded the efforts of women everywhere and told them, "You are doing a noble work." However, when the women petitioned for their own rights, they received little sympathy and much active opposition.

Republicans had declared that suffrage was a natural right belonging to every citizen who paid taxes and helped support the state and that the ballot was the only weapon by which one class could protect itself against the aggressions of another. Despite this, the Republicans failed to help the women in favor of the abolitionist movement. Many abolitionists refused to sign the women's petition, saying, "This is the African American's hour." African American men warned that "women must not block our chance, lumbering the Republican Party with woman suffrage."

Sojourner Truth. Library of Congress

In 1869 when the Fourteenth Amendment was passed, it codified the citizenship of "males" but did not clarify voting rights for citizens or limit those rights to men. Therefore, the Fifteenth Amendment was proposed, providing that "the right of citizens of the United States to vote shall not be denied or abridged by the United States or by any State on account of race, color, or previous condition of servitude." The suffragists made every effort to add "sex" to race and color, but again they were told it was "the African American's hour," and in 1870 the amendment was passed without the word "sex."

In the meantime, many women attempted to vote in local, state, and national elections, claiming that the Fourteenth Amendment established beyond a doubt their citizenship, and that, as citizens, their privileges and immunities, even though not specially guarded as were men's, should not be abridged by any state law limiting the franchise to males. A Mrs. Virginia Minor, of St. Louis, went so far as to bring suit against Reese Happersett, registrar for the election district in which she lived, because he refused to place her name on the list of registered voters. Happersett's defense was that the constitution of Missouri gave suffrage to male citizens only.

The case eventually made its way to the United States Supreme Court, which handed down its decision on in 1875 as follows: (1) that women may be citizens, sex never having been made "one of the elements of citizenship in the United States"; (2) that the Constitution does not define the privileges and immunities of citizens, but that suffrage is not necessarily one of them; (3) that the guaranty of a republican form of government is not a guaranty of universal suffrage; and (4) "that the Constitution of the United States does not confer the right of suffrage upon anyone, and that the constitutions and laws of the several states which commit that important trust to men alone are not necessarily void."

After that decision, some believers in equal suffrage felt there was nothing to do but work for another national amendment to the Constitution. Congress after Congress received petitions, only to throw them into convenient wastepaper baskets. Many of the foremost women in the country pleaded before attentive committees on woman suffrage and judiciary committees for the right to protect their interests and their children's interests.

African American and abolitionist Sojourner Truth campaigned alongside Elizabeth Cady Stanton and Susan B. Anthony against any amendment that denied voting rights to women. At a women's rights convention in Akron, Ohio, in 1851, Miss Truth delivered a moving speech about the issue that has resonated for more than 150 years. In it, she defended women against theological attacks from a group of ministers and railed against discrimination.

"Well, children, whar dar is so much racket there must be something out o' kilter," Miss Truth's speech began. "I think that 'twixt the negroes of the South, and the women at the North, all a talkin' 'bout rights, the white men will be in a fix pretty soon. But what's all this here talking 'bout?

"That man over there says that women needs to be heled into carriages, and lifted ober ditches, and have the best place every whar. Nobody ever helps me into carriages, or ober mud puddles, or gives me any best place! And ain't I a woman? Look at me! Look at my arm! I have plowed and planted, and gathered into barns, and no man could help me! And ain't I a woman? I could work as much and eat as much as a man—when I could get it—and bear the lash as well! And ain't I a woman? I borne thirteen children, and seen most all sold off to slavery, and when I cried out with my mother's grief none but Jesus heard me! And ain't I a woman?

"Then they talk 'bout this thing in the head; what's this they call it? Intellect. That's it, honey. What's that got to do with women's rights or negroes' rights? If my cup won't hold but a pint, an your'n holds a quart, wouldn't you be mean not to let me have my little half-measure full?

"Then that little man in black there, the ministers, he says women can't have as much rights as men, 'cause Christ wasn't a woman! Whar did your Christ come from? From God and a woman! Man had nothing to do with him.

"If the first women God ever made was strong enough to turn the world upside down all 'lone, these women together ought to be able to turn it back, and get it right side up again! And now they is asking to do it—the men better let 'em."

Suffragists owed a substantial debt to the anti-slavery movement which had served as the most important training ground for its leaders and the most important repository for ideas of sexual as well as racial emancipation in the decades before the Civil War, but in the years after the war, former allies set against one another in a new battle that would rage for decades.

their footing on the home front as women were encouraged back into domestic roles were frequently cited as reasons to withhold equal rights. The advances in industrialization that further changed civilization gave rise to the unnamed as yet but deeply held ideals of "true womanhood." When woman suffrage was mentioned in drawing rooms it met with derision, ridicule, a spark of reforming zeal from those who thought women might provide a softening influence on men through the vote, or outright hostility at the thought of women leaving the domestic arena.

Wyoming Territory's motives for extending the vote to women probably had more to do with publicity and attracting female settlers to the territory than with any desire to establish a more egalitarian society. In 1869, men outnumbered women in the Wyoming Territory by a ratio of six to one, and the six thousand adult men who would be part of the decision-making process regarding women's suffrage had a vested interest in growing the territory through the arrival of more women. However, individual men's interests in the idea of women's rights had their roots in diverse ideologies. Some men assumed that wives and mothers would vote with more conservative interests; others assumed that women would vote as their husbands and fathers did; some were pressured by their own wives and mothers; some were motivated by racism and the backlash against the Reconstruction amendments passed in the aftermath of the Civil War.

In Wyoming, territorial legislator William Bright and territorial secretary Edward M. Lee brought their own agendas to the table when they championed the legislation that would eventually become law under Governor John A. Campbell. They also brought the support of women like Esther Hobart Morris, who was championed as the mother of Wyoming women's suffrage and became the first woman justice of the peace in the United States. Wyoming's men may have made the right choice for the wrong reasons, but women were ready to step in and assume their place at last.

FRANK LESLIE'S ILLUSTRATED NEWSPAPER

No. 1,735.—Vol. LXVII.]   NEW YORK—FOR THE WEEK ENDING NOVEMBER 24, 1888.   [PRICE, 10 CENTS.

WOMAN SUFFRAGE IN WYOMING TERRITORY.—SCENE AT THE POLLS IN CHEYENNE.

Frank Leslie's illustrated newspaper featured Wyoming women voting for the first time in a November 1888 issue. Library of Congress

The Politics of Joining the Union

As the delegates to the second Constitutional Congress sat in solemn contemplation of the future of the thirteen colonies that had but recently earned the title of independent states in 1787, they were keenly aware of the vast continent that stretched west unseen to the Pacific Ocean and of the threats posed to the new nation by settlement of that land by other nations. The delegates who drafted the Constitution anticipated the need for the new nation to grow and for the creation of new states as the population grew and settlement stretched to the west. Just over a decade after that momentous convention, then President Thomas Jefferson would orchestrate the biggest land purchase in history, acquiring the 827,000 square miles of the Louisiana Purchase from France in 1803, boggling the imagination and opening up the possibility of growing from thirteen to thirty or more states over time.

And Article IV, Section 3 of the Constitution spelled out the requirements for state's carved from that wide territory to join the Union:

New States may be admitted by the Congress into this Union; but no new State shall be formed or erected within the Jurisdiction of any other State; nor any State be formed by the Junction of two or more States, or Parts of States, without the Consent of the Legislatures of the States concerned as well as of the Congress.

The Congress shall have Power to dispose of and make all needful Rules and Regulations respecting the Territory or other Property belonging to the United States; and nothing in this Constitution shall be so construed as to Prejudice any Claims of the United States, or of any particular State.

The great internal tension of both the Congress that met in 1787 and the document that has guided the nation for more than two hundred years centered on the relationship of the states to each other and the relative power of the federal government. And in the years after Thomas Jefferson effectively doubled the size of the territory of the United States, another underlying tension—how a country that declared all men were created equal could deny rights to Native Americans, enslaved Africans, and women—would in combination with the issue of states' rights precipitate our great Civil War.

After the Confederacy was restored to the Union at the end of the Civil War, the compromise of 1850, which allowed territories to become states only in pairs—one free and one slave—was null and void. Rules were put in place based on population and local government structures that encouraged territories to encourage emigration. Thus in 1869, Wyoming Territory looked at the possibility of encouraging emigration through the publicity of allowing women the right to vote—and by attracting women who took them seriously. And the ongoing conversation about the laws in the new territories left a door open for them to discuss suffrage on a case-by-case basis.

When the territorial legislature met in November 1869, Representative William H. Bright introduced the suffrage measure, which passed. On December 10, 1869, Territorial Governor John A. Campbell made Wyoming famous and earned it the nickname "the Equality State." A grandmother named Louisa Ann Swain became the first American woman to cast a vote in a general election in September 1870, and Esther Morris and seven of her South Pass neighbors also stepped up to the polling place on that historic day. But in spite of the fact that the men's motives in giving women the right to vote may have been suspect, strong women like Louisa Ann Swain and Esther Morris (who became the first woman to serve as justice of the peace in the United States) grabbed the opportunity with both hands and hung on tight.

The tea-party meeting that eventually became famous and earned Morris the nickname "Mother of Women's Suffrage" probably never happened, and though it is likely that she knew Bright because they were both business owners in South Pass, it is even possible that the two had never met officially about the subject before the legislation passed. However, after justice of the peace James W. Stillman resigned in protest after the suffrage bill was signed, Morris was appointed to fill his term in office in February 1870. Though she wasn't a woman with much formal education, Morris demonstrated admirable judgment and restraint in her decisions from the bench, presiding over more than two dozen cases, none of which were overturned on appeal. She also proved that she should be a working woman who still held up her responsibilities as a wife and mother, which helped lead in 1870 to women earning the right to serve on juries in Wyoming Territory. When her term expired, Morris chose not to explore reelection, but her work on behalf of women did not end in South Pass. In 1872, she traveled to San Francisco to attend the American Woman Suffrage Association Convention, and then in 1876 she'd also travel to Philadelphia to the National Suffrage Convention. Susan B. Anthony and other suffrage advocates were quick to point to

Wyoming's successes as they urged legislatures to take up voting rights elsewhere. And when Wyoming became a state, it did so with women's suffrage intact in spite of national opposition. On July 10, 1880, President William Henry Harrison signed a bill admitting Wyoming to the union as the "Equality State." Two weeks later, Morris was honored as a guest at a banquet celebrating the event.

The end of the Civil War, the vast migration of pioneers looking for free land and opportunity on the frontier, and the changing social and economic conditions of the country recovering from war and on the brink of the Gilded Age, plus a little bit of publicity-seeking and opportunism by promoters of the Wyoming Territory, had ushered in a new era for the expansion of women's rights. And as for Esther Morris, her activism and political career didn't end. She served as a delegate to the Republican National Convention in Ohio in 1895. On April 3, 1902, Esther Hobart Morris died in Cheyenne, Wyoming. She was buried there at the Lakeview Cemetery and a simple stone marked her grave. She didn't live to see women get the right to vote nationally and she didn't live to see Nellie Tayloe Ross sworn in as Wyoming's governor in 1925. But her statue now stands in Statuary Hall in the United States Capitol and at the Wyoming State Capitol, a symbol of the important first step taken in favor of women's suffrage in Wyoming.

Human rights took a leap forward when Wyoming opened the polls to women, and Esther Hobart Morris's exemplary tenure as the first woman to hold judicial office in the 1870s did even more. Snickers and snide remarks and motives notwithstanding, the experiment proved that women could participate in the process and hold official posts with success. It would be harder—though not impossible—to argue against extending the franchise in the rest of the West, and then the rest of the country.

CHAPTER TWO

———●●———

Beyond the Overland Trails: Suffrage in Washington and Oregon

If prayer and womanly influence are doing so much for God by indirect methods, how shall it be when that electric force is brought to bear through the battery of the ballot-box?
—FRANCES E. WILLARD, AMERICAN EDUCATOR,
TEMPERANCE REFORMER, AND WOMEN'S SUFFRAGIST

The lines on the elderly woman's face were a roadmap of her life—deeply etched like the wagon tracks that had brought her west to the Oregon Territory in 1852. Under the ornate black hat she wore for the momentous occasion, her face was alight with joy and accomplishment. Abigail Jane Scott Duniway was seventy-eight years old, a pioneer who had crossed the country by wagon train, and a trailblazer for woman suffrage. And she was joyfully, officially casting her vote in an election for the first time. It was 1912, and the voters of Oregon had finally granted Duniway and all of the women of the state suffrage.

By the time Duniway stepped up to make her voice heard at the ballot box for the first time, she had been working tirelessly for the vote for almost half a century. At the age of eighteen, she had emigrated to the territory on the Oregon Trail as part of the Great Migration to settle the West. Traveling with her parents and siblings in 1852, she faced the

Abigail Scott Duniway. Library of Congress

loss of both her mother and a brother on that grueling route. After settling with her remaining family in the small community of Lafayette, she taught school until her marriage to Benjamin Duniway in 1853.

The question of Oregon women's enfranchisement was first asked in 1858 when the idea of the territory becoming a state was being discussed. The census of Oregon taken in the fall of 1859 showed a population of 42,862. Abigail and her family were among those numbered. In addition to woman suffrage, the other items those in the territory were debating were the pending Civil War and slavery.

When Oregon became a state on February 14, 1859, political proponents of statehood refused to consider women who toiled alongside them on the frontier as worthy to vote. According to several articles printed in the *Oregon Argus* newspaper, most men believed "a woman's place was in the home." Abigail Scott Duniway took exception to that notion and made her thoughts known by writing letters to the editor of the publication outlining the importance of women "beyond the confines of the kitchen." Duniway's war against such antiquated ideas and the war waged for woman suffrage in the state were closely tied.

Even as she and her husband took up a homestead and started a family, Duniway started her professional writing career, publishing a novel based on her own experiences in 1859. Shortly after the publication of her book, the family would lose their homestead, making Mrs. Duniway a firsthand witness to how women were unfairly treated when it came to finances and legal matters. There was a piece of property adjoining the farm Ben Duniway owned and subsequently purchased from a widow. The woman was free to sell it because she was a widow, although she signed the legal papers with an X. Abigail knew she had no such rights. According to the law, a woman had no legal claim to her wedding finery, any dowry rights, any claim to property she might inherit after marriage, or any money she might earn. Women were not able to make decisions for themselves in either area.

The reality of such truth would eventually play out in Abigail's own life. In late 1860, Ben entered a business deal she believed would have dire consequences. He signed three notes for a friend. The interest was 2 percent a month, compounded semi-automatically. If the friend could not pay off the notes, Ben would have to. A flood in December 1861 washed away the Duniways' crops as well as the crops of the farmer for whom Ben had signed the notes. The farmer couldn't pay off the notes, and the debt fell to Ben. In a desperate effort to get the money together, Ben went to work in the mines in eastern Oregon. Neither the mines nor the next fall's poor crop brought much of a return. In the fall of 1862, Abigail was handed a summons from the sheriff to pay off the loans. She was furious. "Wives have nothing to say about the notes signed or the farms lost," she wrote in article for the *Oregon Farmer*, "but when the sheriff came, I could receive the summons and be held responsible."

Shortly after Benjamin Duniway risked and lost their property in a bad business deal—a deal entered into without his wife's consent—Benjamin would become permanently disabled, and Abigail found herself the family's main breadwinner. After the unfortunate event, the Duniways moved to Albany. Abigail opened a millinery store there, and Ben cared for the home and the children. Abigail was outspoken about women needing to be regarded as having value in business and civic matters, and she drove home her point in various newspaper articles. Soon women in the area were not just frequenting her shop by buy hats but to complain about the unfair treatment they were experiencing.

A woman came into Abigail's store one day and asked her to go to the courthouse with her. "Courts are for men," Abigail said while preparing to accompany the woman. On the way the woman said, "If I had died first, my husband could have squandered everything that we had accumulated in twenty years. And he would have, too. Now the court is so interested in preserving the property for our children that I can't even buy a shoelace."

At the courthouse, Duniway started to explain the situation as she understood it to the judge. The judge leaned back in his chair and said, "Of course, being ladies, you wouldn't be expected to understand the intricacies of the law."

"No," Duniway shot back, "but we are expected to know enough to foot the bills!"

Duniway's personal experiences influenced her activism. A longtime believer in equal educational rights for female students and a woman with a strong entrepreneurial spirit, in addition to her milliner's shop she ran a boarding school. Abigail believed that not having equal franchise had allowed her husband to lead their family into disaster without her knowledge—and that women who could vote would no longer be that powerless.

Infighting in the Suffrage Movement

In the 1870s, the United States was starting to heal from the wounds of its recent battles. The great Civil War was in the past, and Reconstruction was beginning to settle on the land. An increasingly progressive populist movement was motivated to ratify the Fourteenth and Fifteenth Amendments to the Constitution, and battle lines were being drawn again on the issue of universal suffrage.

The causes of abolition and woman suffrage had long been naturally linked. The women who attended the World Anti-Slavery Convention in London in 1840, including Elizabeth Cady Stanton, were enraged by their exclusion from floor proceedings. They were asked to observe from behind a curtain. But these women, including Quaker women who had long been encouraged to speak their mind in meeting, were frequently seen as champions of reform. And other women followed their example.

In 1848, when Susan B. Anthony and Elizabeth Cady Stanton convened the Seneca Falls Women's Rights Convention, many of the attendees were already vocal advocates for the ending of the "peculiar institution" in the United States. Slavery, though it had been outlawed in England years before, was becoming more entrenched in the American South after the invention of the cotton gin made wide-scale cotton production more profitable. But the fact that slavery was still allowed in Britain's former colony had always stretched the credibility of the new country based on the idea that all men were created equal. The abolition of slavery was first and foremost on the reform-minded brain. Seven women had stepped up to attend the Anti-Slavery Convention in London. Hundreds would declare the rights of women in Seneca Falls and then go right back to work for abolition.

Susan B. Anthony and Elizabeth Cady Stanton. Library of Congress

Temperance—especially the prohibition of alcohol by government —was also a pet cause of many women reformers. They saw the damage that drink could cause in families and advocated for the regulation of intoxicating drink. It quickly became clear, however, that abolition and temperance were not enough to secure women's full rights as citizens. The issues facing women, including the fact that married women couldn't own property or have custody of their children in the event of a divorce, even when they were escaping an abusive husband, were much larger. Women were also not allowed admission to most institutions of learning nor allowed to hold professions. Successful abolition of slavery and prohibition of alcohol aside, women needed the vote to be fully equal.

While the question of slavery was decided during the Civil War, the question of the franchise for recently freed black men and women was not. Allies who had supported each other through the war split almost immediately over the question of whether all freed slaves and all women should immediately earn the franchise or whether that right should only extend to males. Julia Ward Howe, Antoinette Brown, Lucy Stone, and their ally Frederick Douglass believed that guaranteeing the franchise for former male slaves was the priority. They advocated waiting to agitate for woman suffrage. Susan B. Anthony and Elizabeth Cady Stanton vehemently disagreed with that approach—they believed that any delay in gaining the vote for women would stretch on for decades.

Whether or not Stanton and Anthony were correct that pushing for the vote earlier would have gotten it earlier, it would still be decades before national woman suffrage would be enacted. And it would be decades before the rift in the suffrage party—between the former allies of abolitionists and suffragists—would be healed. In the meantime, there was more strife ahead.

As Stanton and Anthony broke from their former supporters, they sought out problematic allies. Both sides suffered under the split, but the progressive suffrage agenda was set back by decades when the suffragists sought the support of Southern racists to defeat suffrage for former male slaves as part of their strategy. The

Lucy Stone. Library of Congress

move would leave a legacy that lingers to this day, but even after the issue of the vote for black men was seemingly settled under the Fourteenth and Fifteenth Amendments, the divisions and lack of coherent strategy within the suffrage movement would hold up the movement even further.

Abigail Scott Duniway's personal-appeal approach to the franchise versus the grander rally-and-speech-and-protest-and-lobby approach marked another division. But the success of the movement in the West may have had more to do with the state-by-state grassroots approach in places where territorial governments were still finding their way and where younger laws proved more malleable. As the vote swept across the West, there were many reasons for its success, but the separation of those campaigns from the controversy of the national movement may have been one of them.

Not long after the episode at the courthouse, Duniway and two other Albany women organized a chapter of the Equal Suffrage Association and wrote for recognition to the society already active in Salem, Oregon. As a result, she attended the California Association meeting in San Francisco. There she was made Oregon correspondent for *The Pioneer*, a women's rights newspaper published in San Francisco. Abigail then began thinking about creating a similar publication in Portland.

Portland was then a town of eight thousand people with three daily newspapers. Nevertheless, the family soon moved there and rented a house. Two upstairs bedrooms of the home were turned into a printing establishment, and a foreman was hired for twenty-five dollars week. The first issue of the (weekly) *New Northwest* newspaper appeared on May 5, 1871.

Journalism was one of the keys to swaying popular opinion about the vote, and with the *New Northwest*, Duniway had a vehicle for publicity. Her paper was filled with news about the suffrage movement from across the country, but it also offered fuel for her larger argument about the need for social and economic equality between men and women. Abigail Duniway's beliefs were being echoed all across the country in the years before and after the Civil War. Families torn apart by violence and by the hardships of forging new lives in the territories often faced difficulties when the surviving female heads of household struggled to provide for their children and dependents. Personal circumstances influenced the politics of women, and the surge toward universal suffrage was changing from ripples to waves. Utah and Wyoming had made the leap. And the western states seemed poised to follow their lead.

By the 1870s, woman suffrage advocates were speaking out at rallies, holding political events, and even protesting publically by attempting to vote in national elections under the argument that the Fourteenth and Fifteenth Amendments gave them that right. Abigail Duniway became known as one of the leading lights of the speaking circuit. She traveled the country on tours to speak about woman suffrage and the rights of women to hold their own property and have equal legal status with men.

In September 1871, Duniway embarked on a tour of Oregon with Susan B. Anthony to help galvanize a woman suffrage crusade. First they went to Salem, then up the Columbia by boat, and by stagecoach as far as Walla Walla. The Duniway family and Miss Anthony went to the Oregon State Fair, camping out on the fairgrounds. Ben and the children returned to Portland, and Abigail and Susan traveled around the Willamette Valley by stage, wagon, carriage, and even by horseback to remote schoolhouses.

Next, they went to Washington Territory, going as far north as Victoria, B.C., where, Abigail reported, the idea of a ballot for women was even more unpopular than in the United States.

They spoke at Olympia, Seattle, Port Townsend, Port Madison, and Port Gamble. The Washington legislature was in session and debating the issue of women's rights when Abigail and Susan arrived in town. When the territorial constitution was drawn up, the men neglected to specify "male" citizens. Some women insisted they were citizens and attempted to vote. The legislature moved to block the oversight. Miss Anthony addressed the assembly, reinforcing the idea, as she had everywhere in the territory, that according to the constitution of the territory women should be allowed to vote.

After Miss Anthony left, a committee of women attended every session of the constitutional congress. A rumor had spread that the debatable suffrage law would be altered or repealed. On the last day, the men suggested the women go home. They would not, they said, tamper with the law.

As the debate about the new Washington State constitution continued, Abigail continued to tour the state of Oregon and speak out for woman suffrage. The speeches she gave were printed in her newspaper. "Gentlemen and Ladies: This large and intelligent audience can bear me witness that our recent defeat in your Legislature has not demoralized us; neither has it in any way diminished our enthusiasm, nor destroyed one iota of confidence in our ultimate triumph," Abigail is quoted as saying in the November 28, 1873, edition of the *New Northwest*. "Indeed, we are stronger now than before the battle as the increasing interest in our cause exhibited by this large attendance abundantly testifies.

"As we have been unable thus far to arouse any opposition in these meetings, and I fear that our opponents are becoming demoralized for the want of a champion to espouse their side of the question, and as I have the reputation of being somewhat of a philanthropist because my sympathies are always with the party that gets the worst of the argument, allow me, for the moment, to assist our enemies in making out a case.

"In rummaging among some old newspapers, at the house of a lady friend, we to-day found a poem entitled 'What are Woman's Rights?' This poem originally appeared in the *Pacific Tribune*, and was suggested, as the introduction states, by the Woman Suffrage Convention held in Olympia two years ago. The author is unknown to me, but the poem reads, in part, as follows:

> *What are woman's rights? you ask me;*
> *I would ask, what are her wrongs?*
> *Does she seek for a position*
> *Which to man alone belongs?*
> *Does she (mourning and complaining)*
> *Tread this beautiful green earth,*
> *Thinking she is right in claiming*
> *Things which ne'er for her had birth?*
> *No true woman seeks to bluster*
> *All her rights or wrongs about—*
> *Something meeker, nobler, higher,*
> *Marks her quiet life throughout.*
> *She will ne'er neglect the blessing*
> *Which will give her greatest joy—*

That for which she has her being,
Watching o'er her infant boy.

"Ladies, I would not abate one jot or tittle of the sentiment contained in this very sentimental effusion. There is a great deal more truth than poetry in it."

Anthony and Duniway's barnstorming tours of the West took some of their momentum from the energetic political reforms and constitutional amendments of the Reconstruction movement and they were feeding the rising unrest among women who suffered personally from disenfranchisement. Abigail Duniway rode the media wave, using the publicity to stir up support for the vote in Oregon and Washington.

In Oregon, however, even though she recognized the benefit of the press's coverage of the need for reforms, Abigail Duniway began to adopt a new strategy—particularly after the defeat of Oregon's first suffrage amendment in 1884. Duniway had come to the conclusion that subtlety—not grandstanding—would eventually win the day. She began a quiet campaign that she called the "still hunt," meeting one-on-one with powerful and influential men in state government. Her instinct told her that personal appeals, which wouldn't attract public opposition, would sway more votes.

In 1887, Duniway closed her newspaper to focus on her new strategy. Unfortunately, she lost credibility with many in the national movement who believed that it would be larger organizations and coalitions like the Women's Christian Temperance Union (WCTU) that would win over voters. Rising to prominence in the last decades of the nineteenth century, the work of the WCTU, founded in 1874, was focused on enacting Prohibition as well as raising awareness of the need for prison reform, labor laws, and eventually suffrage. When the campaign for Prohibition earned the outrage of male tavern owners who fought against both the effort to ban strong drink and the further empowerment of the women advocating for it, the reform work of women was the news of the day—all over the nation.

Duniway would not be swayed from her new approach, however, and she laid the blame for the 1884 defeat of the vote squarely on the WCTU's ability to attract such fervent opposition. Oregon would raise the issue of suffrage on the ballot six times before finally succeeding in 1912.

Duniway didn't contain her efforts to her home state, however. When Idaho, neighbor to Oregon, would become the fourth state in the nation to give women the right to vote, it was with the staunch support and fervent efforts of Abigail Scott Duniway. The right was approved by state legislators in 1896, but not everyone believed the privilege would last. Many miners, businessmen, trappers, and public servants called woman suffrage a "political experiment." According to an article in the December 24, 1896, edition of the *Lewiston Daily Teller*, "the sphere of women should be limited to the home, in the office of wife, mother, and sister, rather than the political arena, wielding the scepter of government."

Almost from the beginning, the notion of women being able to vote in Idaho was tied to Prohibition, as it was in other regions. There was a belief that women would destroy saloons if they had voting power. Suffragists tried to assure lawmakers in Idaho that votes for women would no more prohibit drinking than they would prohibit food. That's not to say that many influential suffragists in the state were uninterested in the issue. Several of the state's most influential suffragists were members of the Woman's Christian Temperance Union. They were against drinking, gambling, and general immorality, but it wasn't a given that giving women access to the ballot would automatically end such behavior.

"I've no quarrel with my friends of the Woman's Christian Temperance Union," Abigail Scott Duniway noted in the speech she gave at the constitution convention. "The most of them, except the professional agitators who make their living out of the business, have agreed with my position since their eyes have been opened by defeat. Quite a number of them no longer wear the little knot of white ribbon, [the] insignia of Pro-hibition, which has the same effect on the average voter when women ask for the ballot as a red rag shaken in the face of an infuriated bull. I love them dearly and respect their sincerity but the equally sincere demands of the majority of women for liberty compel me to speak the truth."

Duniway's analysis of the Prohibition problem and voting rights resulted in the solid backing of many leading state officials and business-men to place suffrage on the ballot. The woman suffrage movement in Idaho gathered together supporters of the best talent and ability in the state. It was then carried on by some of the women of high social posi-tion and aided and abetted by men of eminent talents and responsibili-ties. Among the prominent state senators who helped move suffrage to the ballot were J. M. Bennett from Owyhee County, Frank Wyman of Ada County, and E. H. Dewey of Cassia County. It wasn't until after the legis-lature voted to allow the matter to come before the people at the general election that supporters of the movement feared they had a difficult time on their hands. They had to overcome the inertia more than the opposi-tion of the people. Indifference proved to be more an obstacle than any-thing else. Only a few of the more sanguine advocates of the measure really expected the measure to pass. They thought they would get a good vote but relied on time and education to win the victory when it should come.

The editor and staff at *The Weiser Signal*, one of Idaho's most respected newspapers, predicted that suffrage would fail. "Some of Weiser's best women are becoming frightened over the woman suffrage planks in the platforms and are already expressing their dread that it will be forced upon them," the September 30, 1896, edition of the *Elmore Bulletin* read. "They need not fear. It will be defeated at the polls. It was put in by the Republicans as a political move—to extend the party machinery—and the Democrats, without its being endorsed by the rank and file of the party, thought they had to follow suit to stand them off. Seventy percent of political chicanery, twenty-nine percent of sentiment

Women Need Apply: Job Opportunities in the Wild West

When Susan B. Anthony and Abigail Scott Duniway stood before the Women's Rights Convention in Olympia, Washington, in 1871, they were joined by three women who had come west as "Mercer Girls," young women recruited by Asa Shinn Mercer to come to the Pacific Northwest to work as teachers—and as prospective brides for the men who made up the vast majority of the population in Washington Territory. Women went west for a variety of reasons during the Great Migration of the nineteenth century, coming along with husbands and fathers, but also traveling solo for reasons that included job opportunities, homesteads in some places where they were allowed for single women, and the prospect of more freedom.

Myth and the historical record both place women in professions in the West, where there were shortages of doctors, dentists, lawyers, and journalists, when they might have been denied those same opportunities in the East. Bethenia Owens-Adair, for example, emigrated to Oregon with her family as a small child and then returned to the East to go to medical school, eventually setting up a practice in Portland, Oregon, where she participated in the suffrage movement in the 1880s. Martha Hughes Cannon was a doctor in Salt Lake City in the 1890s, when she also ran for—and won—a seat in the Utah legislature. May Arkwright Hutton went west to the silver camps of Idaho where she started out as a cook in a mining town and became a silver tycoon and philanthropist in her own right. Other women went west to be singers, other performers, photographers, social workers, restaurateurs, scouts, and homesteaders—as well as to take up less savory professions and to be mail-order brides.

Perhaps because educated women went west to practice their careers, perhaps because the mere fact that they were pioneers gave them the conviction that anything was possible, and perhaps because the nascent governments of the West offered pathways to reform that were simply more straightforward than those in more established states, the reforming zeal swept across the West, and by 1920, when the Nineteenth Amendment was ratified, the women of the West were already voting.

and one of wisdom is what really brought forth three planks this year in three parties which not one of the parties will endorse. The amendment will surely be defeated."

Idaho covered some 83,569 square miles, and many of the counties at the time could not be reached by railroad. Political campaigning was a rugged venture. Women who had a heart for the cause canvassed the state by walking or riding horseback. Suffragists were often permitted to speak from the same stand with the orators of the various political parties. They did not take sides with either of the parties in the state that were contending for the victory but devoted their energies to persuading the people of the benefits and justices of women suffrage.

The suffragists canvassing Idaho had little money to devote to their efforts. Less than $500 was spent by them in the entire campaign. Most of the money raised was spent for literature. They had printed fifty thousand posters bearing the words "Vote for the Woman Suffrage Amendment," and those posters were sent to every precinct in the state. The local club in Boise had three thousand facsimiles of the suffrage amendment printed and circulated at the polls. Some of the voters did not understand that the facsimiles were a promotional tool and voted on them instead of the actual ballots. When all the ballots were in, the official count showed the amendment had received 12,126 votes in its favor and 6,282 against.

"This placed in our constitution and in our statute-books a suffrage law of the most absolute and sweeping character," Governor Frank Steunenberg wrote in *Harper's Bazaar* in 1900. "It placed both sexes on an exact equality, not only so far as voting is concerned, but also in holding office. There is no limitation of the suffrage to school and certain other public functions in which women are specially concerned, as is the case in some states, but the right to vote is universal, for municipal and county officers, state officers, senators and representatives in Congress, state legislators, and for presidential electors. The same equal privilege is open to hold office under the state, county, or municipality government."

On July 3, 1890, Idaho entered the Union as the forty-third state. Eighty-eight thousand citizens resided in Idaho at the time. In May 1900, Governor Steunenberg noted in an editorial for *Harper's Bazaar* that the origin of the suffrage movement in the legislature was spontaneous and not the result of any particular or prolonged outside propaganda to spread the practice or doctrine of suffrage for women. "In a community of liberal and progressive ideas the time seemed ripe for giving to women an equal share with men in the conduct of public affairs," Governor Steunenberg commented about Idaho granting women the vote. "Without special effort, and with practically no opposition, the legislature adopted the joint resolution submitting the question to the people. Once this had been done, the women throughout the state were stimulated to exertion; systematic organization was perfected in the state and counties, and an active campaign inaugurated."

The 1898 election was the first in which Idaho women could vote. In that election, the first female statewide office holder was elected, Permeal French, a Democratic state superintendent of public instruction who served until 1903.

To the north, Washington had first considered suffrage as part of its formation as a territory, and in 1854, the first territorial legislature considered a woman's suffrage clause as part of its constitution—a clause that failed by only one vote more than a decade before Wyoming Territory would grant its female citizens the franchise. When in 1867, while Reconstruction was forcing the issue nationally, the legislature passed a law granting the right to vote to "all white citizens above the age of 21" many early woman suffrage proponents leapt on it as further evidence that the Fourteenth Amendment applied to women's citizenship and thus voting rights.

After Susan B. Anthony, Abigail Scott Duniway, and other notable suffragists rallied for the vote in Washington in 1871, the territorial legislature again failed to pass a proposed suffrage bill by a slim margin, but the campaign had two effects: the formation of multiple suffrage organizations across the territory and the rejection of the women's lobbying efforts in the form of a bill that declared loudly that women in the territory would not be able to vote until the U.S. Congress passed suffrage nationally. The events there gave Duniway even more evidence for her belief that the public campaign could do more harm than good to the cause.

In fact, during the decade before Washington territory would become a state, the issue of suffrage was raised again and again. Territorial laws had allowed women to vote in school elections, though not consistently. In 1877, two years after another wider suffrage bill had failed, the territorial legislature ratified tax-paying women's right to vote in school elections. The men who first inhabited Washington Territory and shaped the initial political structure of the area made views about woman suffrage clear when they mandated that "no female shall have the right of ballot or vote." In 1869, that directive was challenged by Olympia resident Mary Olney Brown with the support of legislator Edward Eldridge. The territorial law noted that for one to vote they must be a white American over the age of twenty-one. Brown and Eldridge argued that because Mary fit the criteria she was therefore legally entitled to vote in the territory of Washington. Mary was not able to persuade legislators to let her cast her ballot, but she did persuade election judges in two Washington precincts to recognize women's right to vote based on the wording of the territorial law.

That same year the legislature passed the territory's first community property law, which gave women joint legal ownership of any property owned by either themselves or their husbands after marriage. The lawmakers' actions strengthened the legal status for women. Brown's challenge, coupled with the approval of the new community property law, helped lay the groundwork for the woman suffrage movement in the territory. Mary Olney Brown continued to play a part in the quest for suffrage in Washington. She lobbied for a woman suffrage clause to be added to the new constitution scheduled to be drafted at the constitutional convention in Walla Walla in 1878. In addition to circulating petitions throughout the territory, Brown wrote editorials for newspapers to educate both men and women about the issue. The constitutional convention was comprised of sixteen men, one of the smallest conventions of its kind held in the United States. Abigail Duniway was given the opportunity to speak to the sixteen men about woman suffrage. In her speech, she appealed to the delegates to "grant women her rightful place beside you in the new constitution of the new state, which you are to christen Washington, and forthwith your new born commonwealth shall become a star of the first magnitude." However, a women's suffrage clause was excluded from the proposed constitution by a vote of seven to eight. For those women dedicated to the cause, the fight continued. A great deal of work had to be done to convince Washington Territory residents that the sphere of womanhood extended beyond the doorsteps of her home and that women should have the right to represent themselves at the polling booth. Women wanted their views on such issues as slavery, prostitution, gambling, and alcohol to be respected.

The zeal numerous women felt for the cause after the convention in 1871 had dissipated considerably by the fall of 1883. Many women had allowed themselves to be intimidated by detractors who insisted that lobbying for women's rights was unfeminine. It was Duniway's visit to Olympia in October 1883 that revitalized the suffrage community in the region. She had come to the city to lobby the legislature for woman suffrage. Interest in women voters caught the attention of eastern Washington farmers on the legislature who believed women voters would help "clean up the morals of the territory."

In 1883, both houses of the Washington Territorial Legislature would finally pass women's suffrage, and Territorial Governor William

Newell signed the bill. As Wyoming and Utah knew, however, territorial grant of rights was no guarantee for the future. And for the next two decades, the women of Washington and Oregon fought for their rights to be codified in state law.

Anxious to exercise their new right, women across the state voted in the territorial elections in 1884. According to the November 21, 1884, edition of the *Seattle Post-Intelligencer*, more women reported to the polls than men. As the farmers on the legislature hoped, women voted against corrupt politicians and for Prohibition.

Women's right to vote in Washington Territory turned out to be a short-lived exercise. Influential individuals with gambling and alcohol interests feared that women would continue to harm their business and, in turn, harm the territory's chances to become a state. By August 1888, woman suffrage had been rescinded.

May Arkwright Hutton, Washington delegate to the Democratic National Convention, 1912. Library of Congress

Women in Washington were dispirited and lacked the enthusiasm to mount another big campaign to gain the vote. Tacoma suffragist Emma Smith DeVoe wanted to do something about women's waning fervor and decided to attend the National American Woman Suffrage Association convention in Portland, Oregon, in June 1905, in search of help. Several hundred women from throughout the Northwest were in attendance. The vigorous speeches and powerful debates lit a fire in DeVoe, and she took that fire back to Washington. Her enthusiasm sparked a new suffrage campaign. May Arkwright Hutton, a philanthropist and silver-mine tycoon, picked up the mantle of leadership by 1906, and by 1909, Washington women were ready to put an amendment to the state constitution to a vote. Following the lead of Abigail Scott Duniway, DeVoe and Hutton moved their efforts to offices and drawing rooms rather than rallies and speeches, lobbying supporters individually and not drawing the ire of the anti-suffrage vote. The wives, mothers, sisters, and daughters of men who voted worked on a personal basis to influence the vote.

Women's clubs across the state joined DeVoe in her efforts to regain support from discouraged suffragists. Funds were raised to advance the cause, and new petitions were circulated. To drum up the vote, the women distributed cookbooks. Newspapers held "kitchen contests" to stimulate interest. One hardy group of mountaineer females climbed their weary way to the summit of Mt. Rainier near Tacoma, lugging an immense banner which they unfurled on the very peak. The banner, which read "Give Women the Vote," could not be seen from a distance, but the grand gesture served to inspire others to get involved. "The goal of DeVoe and the other suffragettes was solid," an article in the June 29, 1905, edition of the *East Oregonian* noted. "The ideal and aim was a government of men and women—not by women alone, not by men alone, but a government of men and women."

Emma DeVoe and Senator George Cotterill drafted the woman suffrage bill introduced in the legislature in January 1909. According to

Emma Smith DeVoe. Library of Congress

the January 29, 1909, edition of the *Seattle Star*, the bill vote passed with seventy for and eighteen opposing. Several fervid "God Bless You" speeches for ladies were made once the bill went through. "It is time women should be able to vote," an editorial in the March 5, 1909, edition of the *Seattle Times* read. "Men haven't always agreed that women in Washington should have the right, but a broad conscientious study of the principles involved must bring any thoughtful, fair, unbiased mind to this conclusion."

Eventually, the measure that would amend the Washington Constitution to grant the franchise to women won by a vote of nearly two to one—every county was in favor. In November 1910, women in Washington exercised in full their newly acquired right, voting in the same proportion as men and setting their sights on moral reform.

The first state to ratify woman suffrage in the twentieth century, Washington State followed the example of the western states of Wyoming, Utah, Colorado, and Idaho in 1910. California would be next, granting its daughters the right to vote in 1911. And then in 1912, Oregon, which had long been a partner to Washington in the fight for the franchise, finally took the final steps that allowed Abigail Scott Duniway the chance to stand at the ballot box, the first woman to register to vote in Oregon after suffrage passed in the state in 1913. The former schoolteacher, journalist, and author fought more than half her life for women to have the right to vote. As the years passed, Duniway had gained increasing recognition as the foremost women's rights leader in the West. She succeeded in getting women's suffrage before the Oregon legislature six times between 1884 and 1912, each time gaining a few more votes. The suffrage bill in Oregon passed in November 1912, with a vote of 61,265 for and 57,104 against. When the bill finally became law, Governor Oswald West asked Duniway to write the proclamation and gave her the pen with which he signed the bill.

Abigail Scott Duniway writing the equal suffrage proclamation for Oregon that Governor Oswald West stands ready to sign. Library of Congress

Duniway's autobiography, written in 1914 and entitled *Path Breaking*, closes with the following paragraph: "The young women of today—free to speak, to write, to choose their occupation should remember that every inch of their freedom was bought with a great price. It is for them to show their gratitude by helping onward the reforms of their own time by spreading the light of freedom and truth still wider. The debt that each generation owes to the past it must pay to the future."

Abigail Scott Duniway died on October 11, 1915, five years prior to the passage of the Nineteenth Amendment, prohibiting the states and the federal government from denying the right to vote to citizens of the United States on the basis of sex.

By the time of this Washington, D.C., parade in 1913, women in Oregon, Utah, and Idaho already had the franchise. They wore their sashes as examples in their support for women's right to vote. Author's Collection

CHAPTER THREE

The Pride of Colorado:
Silver and Suffrage

Those who are ruled by law should have the power to say what shall be the laws, and who the lawmakers will be. Women are as much interested in legislation as men and are entitled to representation.
—WILLIAM LLOYD GARRISON, AMERICAN ABOLITIONIST, JOURNALIST, SUFFRAGIST, AND SOCIAL REFORMER

It was a typical Colorado October evening, one of those days when a promising crisp and sunny morning had turned dark and windy by late afternoon. In spite of the rain and bluster, however, a crowd was gathering in the Union Hall on Pearl Street to hear the legendary Susan B. Anthony address the subject of woman suffrage. It was 1877, and the creation of Colorado's one-year-old state constitution was still fresh in its citizen's memories. And both women and men were asking the question: Why shouldn't Colorado follow Wyoming and Utah's example and extend universal suffrage to the so-called "fairer sex?"

Anthony was, by that time, a veteran of the fight for women's rights in the United States, a former champion of the abolitionist movement, and a fierce proponent of the right to vote for all citizens. In 1872, after the ratification of the Fourteenth and Fifteenth Amendments to the

Constitution, she and a group of her sisters and friends had registered to vote in Rochester, New York, arguing that the Fourteenth Amendment gave them that right. The women were then arrested for casting their ballots. Anthony was held on $1,000 bail and was then fined $100 for casting her vote. And Anthony was only one of the many women who had been fighting since the 1840s to have their voices heard. Across the country, women had been agitating for the vote and making allies of men. And in the West, at least, it seemed that men were listening. In Utah and Wyoming, the writers of the territorial constitutions had recognized the political expediency of enfranchisement for women, and in Colorado, the topic was ripe for debate.

Scarcely a month before Colorado officially became a state on August 1, 1876, the citizens of Denver had gathered for a grand Fourth of July celebration, an event that seemed especially significant in that centennial year. Parades and toasts included stirring words about the role of women in the state, and one speaker solemnly intoned, "May there yet be had a fuller recognition of her social influence, her legal identity and her political rights." The pressure for the state to allow women the vote was growing.

In fact, as early as 1870, Territorial Governor Edward McCook had proposed the idea of following the example of Wyoming Territory and extending the full franchise to the women of Colorado. His efforts were rebuffed, but the notion had caught the attention of the men who were elected to take the state through the process of writing the constitution five years later. Delegates Henry P. Bromwell of Denver and Agipeto Vigil from Huerfano and Las Animas Counties proposed that equal suffrage be included in the state constitution, but were outvoted when the constitution came to a vote in 1876, limiting women's right to vote to school elections.

The next year, however, a referendum on the issue went before the male voters of the state asking to grant the franchise to the women who worked and lived alongside them, and the historic move brought luminaries of the national suffrage movement to the Rocky Mountains. Henry

Blackwell and Lucy Stone joined Susan B. Anthony in stumping across the state. Local suffragists such as Matilda Hindman and Margaret Campbell were joined by former territorial governor John Evans in encouraging their fellow Coloradans to vote yes on the measure that November.

Elsewhere across the country—and especially across the West—women's clubs were organizing on the ground, waging campaigns of personal persuasion and focusing their arguments on the local ills that suffragists proposed would be remedied by just giving women the right to vote. Suffrage advocates didn't just want the vote because they believed in the right. They wanted the vote to help put laws into action that would promote health and welfare reforms for women and children, help abused women leave abusive husbands without losing custody of their children, and help women hold the rights to their own property. In Colorado in 1877, however, fast on the heels of statehood, the time was seemingly not ripe for the vote.

During the 1870s and 1880s, the state-by-state approach to the franchise seemed to stall. Ballot measure after ballot measure was introduced across the United States, and particularly in the West where territories were forming state governments and joining the Union. As women's groups rose in prominence, their focus shifted from a single-minded drive for the vote to Prohibition and other popular progressive causes. Factions in the women's movement that arose both from postwar politics and differences over tactics further slowed a national push for the vote. Voting rights in the East still seemed a distant dream, but the success of Utah and Wyoming suffrage was an inspiration to women's groups and to male-led legislatures, especially in the West. Colorado's 1877 attempt to pass a suffrage bill had demonstrated that a two-prong approach—grassroots efforts combined with national attention—had the potential to succeed there.

By 1890, the National Woman Suffrage Association and the American Woman Suffrage Association had set aside their differences and merged to form the National American Woman Suffrage Association, the

Ellis Meredith: Journalist, Suffragist, Activist

Ellis Meredith was the daughter of pioneers. Born in Montana Territory in 1865, she was the daughter of Emily R. Meredith, a well-known advocate for woman suffrage, and Frederick Allison, a journalist. The family had been drawn to the gold-rush boomtown and territorial capital of Bannack, Montana, living there for a couple of years before Ellis's birth. Later they would return to Minnesota, where her mother had attended Hamline University and her father had been the editor of the *Red Wing Republican*.

In 1885, the family moved to Denver, Colorado, where Ellis's father was the managing editor of the Rocky Mountain News for a time, and where her mother worked as a journalist. Ellis followed in their footsteps early, writing for the *Rocky Mountain News* on her favorite subjects: women's rights and the temperance movement.

In 1893, Ellis traveled to Chicago for the World's Exposition, where she met with Susan B. Anthony on the eve of Colorado's granting of woman suffrage. Already prominent in Colorado politics because of her activism on women's issues, ten years later, Ellis was elected as a delegate to the Denver City Charter Convention, and then became a member of the Colorado Democratic Party State Central Committee and a city election commissioner.

Local politics were not Ellis's only interest. She lent her support to the national campaign for women's suffrage in 1904, speaking in front of the U.S. House of Representatives and calling for the amendment of the Constitution to provide women the right to vote. In 1917, she would find herself working in Washington, D.C., at the national Democratic headquarters three years before the ratification of suffrage.

Ellis Meredith would live to see women vote nationwide, both world wars, and the start of the Cold War, dying at age ninety in November 1955. Her drive to ensure the rights of women earned her the nicknames "The Susan B. Anthony of Colorado" and the "symbol of the Progressive West."

NAWSA. Though the national organization began campaigns all over the country, it was demographics and economics that helped Colorado's 1893 referendum pass—making it the first state to grant universal suffrage to women through popular vote.

A small group of stalwart local reformers, organized as the Colorado Non-Partisan Equal Suffrage Association, were responsible for the referendum and the campaign. From the start, the group had some popular support—including a group of women in southern Colorado who had organized opposition to their anti-suffrage state senator—and they had political endorsers as well, including Governor Davis Waite and former governor John Routt. The nonpartisan nature of their campaign was evident in its supporters—Waite was a populist, while Routt was a Republican.

Brewery owners and saloonkeepers were often the most serious opposition that suffragists faced. The fear that women voters would use their franchise to close down the liquor business inspired much of the anti-suffrage rhetoric in the West. Perhaps because of the larger economic forces at work—and perhaps because of the wide and growing press support, the tavern associations didn't mount much of an opposition. Their last-minute campaign failed to include the support of the barmaids and prostitutes who plied their trade in the saloons, most of whom supported suffrage or were at least sympathetic to the cause.

The press was an ally, however. Of forty-four newspapers in the state, only eleven were opposed—officially—to woman suffrage. At the *Rocky Mountain News*, Ellis Meredith and Minnie J. Reynolds, two of the paper's columnists, were vocal supporters of suffrage. The publisher, Thomas Patterson, however, was opposed to the measure sponsored by Representative J. T. Heath of Montrose County, so officially the paper was neutral. Activist Elizabeth Ensley rallied African American (male) support in the cities while Grange women organized farmers on the eastern plains. They all argued that working people's needs, especially those of women and children, were being ignored by mainstream politicians.

Women voters, they felt, might fix inadequate schools, squalid housing conditions, unhealthy working conditions, and clean up Colorado's dirty politics. Women and men stood and spoke in churches, marched door-to-door in mining towns, and barnstormed farming communities across the state, crying "Let the women vote! They can't do any worse than the men!"

Demographically the state of Colorado had changed since its earliest days as a mining territory. The silver rush had brought large numbers of white miners to the state—and the whites far outnumbered the Hispanic male voters who had helped defeat the referendum in 1877. Some men in that anti-immigrant mindset might have considered that if white women were given the right to vote, their voices would outnumber those of people of color. Further, since 70 percent of women over the age of nineteen were married, the small number of single and divorced women who would be counted on to vote outside the bounds of a secure domestic relationship was small enough to be discounted politically.

Colorado journalists and writers and other professionals played an important part in the campaign for suffrage. Minnie Reynolds's voice at the *Rocky Mountain News* was joined by that of novelist Patience Stapleton. And a group of women physicians—Dr. Ethel Strasser, Dr. Anna Chamberlain, and Dr. Jessie Hartwell—worked with Denver teacher Martha A. Pease to construct a campaign that demonstrated women's intellectual ability to vote. No argument was deemed too feeble. The cause was also helped by the wealthy and privileged in Denver society. Mrs. Nathanial P. Hill and Elizabeth "Baby Doe" Tabor, wife of Horace Tabor, the so-called "Silver King" donated both their status and their fortunes to assist in what ended up being a six thousand-vote win over the opposition that fall.

The referendum that would go to a vote on November 7, 1893—HB 118— had been drafted by a Denver lawyer named J. Warner Mills and was sponsored in the legislature by Representative J. T. Heath. Church

The Fourteenth and Fifteenth Amendments

For decades—since even before the signing of the Declaration of Independence—the country that would become the United States of America had been torn apart over the issue of slavery. For four years the fight had ripped families apart and threatened to end all that had made the United States develop and grow, and then Reconstruction—the set of laws and measures put into place to bring the two halves of a divided country together—threatened to divide the nation further as Southern states resisted what they considered to be draconian measures leveled against them. Few issues were as contentious as the fate of the formerly enslaved, particularly their citizenship and right to vote. And the so-called Reconstruction amendments, laboriously debated and grudgingly ratified, were a critical step forward to resolve the question of the future of former slaves as free people.

A celebration of the Fifteenth Amendment, May 19, 1870. Library of Congress

Adopted in July 1868, the Fourteenth Amendment to the U.S. Constitution was intended to address the issue of citizenship of former slaves in the aftermath of abolition and as a part of allowing the Southern states to rejoin the union. Suffragists would aim their legal argument for the vote at the first section of the amendment, which specified persons and citizens, not sex:

Section 1. All persons born or naturalized in the United States, and subject to the jurisdiction thereof, are citizens of the United States and of the State wherein they reside. No State shall make or enforce any law which shall abridge the privileges or immunities of citizens of the United States; nor shall any State deprive any person of life, liberty, or property, without due process of law; nor deny to any person within its jurisdiction the equal protection of the laws.

However, Section 2 of the amendment carefully described the consequences of failing to allow men the right to vote, stymieing their argument. Section 1 seemed clear. Women were citizens. Section 2 carefully described what would happen if men were denied the right to vote.

Section 2. Representatives shall be apportioned among the several States according to their respective numbers, counting the whole number of persons in each State, excluding Indians not taxed. But when the right to vote at any election for the choice of electors for President and Vice President of the United States, Representatives in Congress, the Executive and Judicial officers of a State, or the members of the Legislature thereof, is denied to any of the male inhabitants of such State, being twenty-one years of age, and citizens of the United States, or in any way abridged, except for participation in rebellion, or other crime, the basis of representation therein shall be reduced in the proportion which the number of such male citizens shall bear to the whole number of male citizens twenty-one years of age in such State.

Two years later, in 1870, the ratification of the Fifteenth Amendment clarified the issue of voting for former slaves:

Section 1. The right of citizens of the United States to vote shall not be denied or abridged by the United States or by any State on account of race, color, or previous condition of servitude.

Section 2. The Congress shall have power to enforce this article by appropriate legislation.

To the advocates of woman suffrage who had been working toward their goal for years, the words of Section 1 meant one thing: States couldn't infringe on the right of any person, male or female, who wanted to vote. The problem with the argument was Section 2, which kept women from voting for another five decades. Male-controlled state legislatures generally held that the whole amendment was only meant to apply to adult men. And there were plenty of laws on the books at the state level to keep women down. Susan B. Anthony would be arrested in 1872 for attempting to vote in a presidential election even as women in Wyoming were exercising their franchise for the first time.

VOL. XXXV. No. 900.   PUCK BUILDING, New York, June 6th, 1894.
Copyright, 1894, by Keppler & Schwarzmann.

A SQUELCHER FOR WOMAN SUFFRAGE.
HOW CAN SHE VOTE, WHEN THE FASHIONS ARE SO WIDE, AND THE VOTING BOOTHS ARE SO NARROW?

Supporters of woman suffrage sometimes faced snide commentary from their opponents, including this 1893 cover of Puck *magazine that claimed women's fashion would keep them from voting, even as more and more frontier states extended the franchise to the "fairer sex."* Library of Congress

groups, political parties, women's charities, unions, and farmers groups joined with the Colorado Non-Partisan Equal Suffrage Association to make the success of the election possible. In the end, more than thirty-five thousand residents voted in favor of the referendum with fewer than thirty thousand against. The next day, the headline beneath journalist and suffragist Caroline Nichols Churchill's byline cried, "Western Women Wild with Joy over Colorado's Election."

In Colorado, as in the rest of the United States, gaining the franchise did not result in an immediate shift of political power. In 1894, three women would be elected to the Colorado House of Representatives. Clara Cressingham, Carrie Clyde Holly, and Frances Klock were the first women to serve constituencies in a state legislature. Even though women were almost immediately elected to the legislature following the granting of the vote, the notorious "old boys' network" still pulled most of the levers. The small female minority in any political body meant that women's issues still took a low priority. Eventually, however, with the help of women, Colorado would become the first state to outlaw the sale of liquor—something the brewers and tavern owners probably regretted. But women had many more important roles in improving the lives of their sisters and fellow Coloradans. Between 1899 and 1912, women helped shape more than 150 state statutes. Some, like making the columbine the state flower, were symbolic. Others protected the rights of women and children by barring pimps from taking their prostitutes' profits and setting up a juvenile court. Women were also given the right to homestead and to have the same privileges accorded to other heads of house if they were their family's chief support.

CHAPTER FOUR

Twice Won:
Woman Suffrage in Utah

The correct principle is that women are not only justified, but
exhibit the most exalted virtue, when they enter on the concerns
of their country, of humanity, and of their God.

—JOHN QUINCY ADAMS,
SIXTH PRESIDENT OF THE UNITED STATES

On April 5, 1895, the lavish Grand Opera House in Salt Lake
City was filled to overflowing with a host of well-dressed ladies
and gentlemen. Women engaged in serious discussions outnumbered
the men filtering into the building. Musicians in the orchestra pit ser-
enaded the preoccupied crowd standing, talking, and preparing to sit
upon rows of waiting chairs. As the clock approached two o'clock in the
afternoon, more than a dozen women filtered on stage and took their
places among the plush seats stationed in front of a magnificent, hand-
painted drop curtain. Conversations quieted, and the room slowly came
to order. When the music faded, Mrs. J. A. Froiseth called the meeting
of suffragists in the Utah Territory to order. The following articles were
read to the audience.

"Whereas, a convention is being held in this city for the purpose of framing a constitution for the proposed state of Utah, and; whereas, the question is being considered by said convention of incorporating in said constitution a provision for women suffrage, and; whereas, no opportunity has been afforded the women of this Territory to manifest their opinion upon the matter; and whereas, by the adoption of a plank of favor of woman suffrage in the platforms of both political parties, no opportunity was afforded to the citizens of this Territory to indicate their approval or disapproval of the proposition, and; whereas, it is conceded alike by the advocates and the opponents of woman suffrage that in all intellectual attributes and attainments the women are entitled to vote, and if this is true, then they possess the necessary intelligence and attainments to enable them to determine for themselves whether they desire this privilege, and they should be given the opportunity to decide this question for themselves."

The crowd of onlookers cheered and applauded the articles read aloud. They waved their hands in the air approvingly and congratulated one another for their dedication to the cause. Someone shouted, "Give me suffrage or give me nothing." That single voice then led many in a chant of "Give me suffrage or give me nothing!"

An enthusiastic supporter of the cause leapt to her feet and proclaimed, "The fight is still on!" Fellow believers praised the sentiment. "Ninety percent of the people hesitate to try the experiment these men would force upon us," the spontaneous orator announced. "You who propose to vote against statehood make your voice heard now, with no uncertain sound. If we are to have equal suffrage, let us have it equal. Let the women serve on juries, let them work their poll tax on the roads, make them subject to military service, let them be drafted and enlisted in time of war, let them be equal in all things!"

More than twenty-five years prior to the enthusiastic gathering at the Grand Opera House where women argued for their right to vote, a somber group of leaders in the Utah Territorial Legislature quietly passed an act giving women that entitlement. Sarah Young, grandniece of settler and Mormon Church leader Brigham Young, became the first women to vote in the region. She voted in a municipal election on February 14, 1869.

Twenty woman leaders of the Mormon Church including Bethseba Smith, Phoebe Woodruff, Zina Diantha Huntington Young, Sarah M. Kimball, and Emmeline B. Wells, 1883. Library of Congress

The decision granting women the opportunity to cast a ballot came with little fanfare to the Utah Territory. The idea was promoted by a group who had parted ways with the Mormon Church. Known as the Godbeites, named after the spiritual leader and protégé of Brigham Young, William S. Godbe, they opposed the regulation of wealth, the avoidance of mining for precious metals, the institution of polygamy, and several other issues they felt hampered Utah's cultural and economic progress. Suffragists in the East hoping to advance their cause beyond the Mississippi were anti-polygamists as well—both factions believed if women in Utah could vote they would vote to end plural marriage.

Women loyal to the Mormon faith made it known they approved of the practice. They wanted the right to vote but were not interested in sacrificing religious practices in exchange. Mormon women viewed polygamy as liberating. Rather than being looked upon as personal property and merely subservient to a man's physical needs, pluralistic marriages offered all women the chance to be honored wives and mothers with a home and a sense of belonging and purpose.

Ultimately, the majority of Utah politicians were persuaded to grant women the right to vote, in hopes it would correct the idea that women in the territory were downtrodden and oppressed.

Leaders of the church like George Q. Cannon, chief political strategist to Brigham Young, approved of elevating women's societal position. "With women to aid in the great cause of reform, what wonderful changes can be affected!" he noted in the February 10, 1869, edition of the *Deseret News Weekly*. "Without her aid how slow the progress! Give her responsibility, and she will prove that she is capable of great things; but deprive her of opportunities, make a doll of her, leave her nothing to occupy her mind but the reading of novels, gossip, the fashions and all the frivolity of the frivolous age, and her influence is lost, and instead of being a helpmate to a man as originally intended, she becomes a drag

Dr. Martha Hughes Cannon is famous as the first woman who was ever sent to a state senate to represent the citizens of a commonwealth. She served four years in the legislature of Utah. She was a woman with a history, and a striking one. Prior to her marriage, she studied medicine under physicians in Salt Lake City, then went to Ann Arbor where she graduated in 1880, and afterward entered the University of Pennsylvania. One hundred twenty-five men started in the auxiliary course with Dr. Cannon, but only five of those and she graduated in 1882.

On her return to Salt Lake City, Dr. Cannon became a resident physician in the Deseret Hospital. She held that position for three years in addition to maintaining a practice outside the hospital. In 1884, she became the sixth wife of Mr. Angus M. Cannon.

Martha Hughes Cannon. Library of Congress

Dr. Cannon's husband was president of the high priest council, which is the ecclesiastical court of jurisdiction in the Mormon Church.

Dr. Cannon firmly believed that women should have the right to vote and spoke out publicly in support of the suffrage movement. She served as Utah delegate at the Columbian Exposition in Chicago and delivered several political and economic stump speeches on the contributions women had made and would continue to make.

Martha Cannon was instrumental in making sure women's enfranchisement was added into Utah's constitution when it was granted statehood in 1896. The same year Utah became a state, she ran against five other candidates in a race for Senate. One of those candidates was her husband. Martha Cannon won the vote in November 1896 and, in so doing, became the first elected female senator in the United States.

and an encumbrance. Such women may answer in other places and among other people, but they would be out of place here."

On February 12, 1870, the Utah Territorial Legislature approved a resolution that would allow the vote to all women over the age of twenty-one. If suffragists in other parts of the country were at all hopeful political leaders in the nation's capital would soon follow Utah's example, they changed their minds after reading an article in the February 15, 1870, edition of the *Brooklyn Daily Eagle*. "There has been lively discussion here [Washington, D.C.] about the adoption of female suffrage in Utah," the news story began. "Never was anything, about which there had been any agitation, more completely and conclusively dead than Woman Suffrage here in Washington. It is as dead as the National Intelligencer—more dead in fact, because that vulnerable sect may be reconstructed, but the Suffrage cannot.

"The feminine spouters who were here not long ago talked in vain, except so far as they found pleasure in the mere act of talking. They accomplished nothing. It is regarded as singular that simultaneously with its failure here is announced the success of the suffrage scheme of Utah. You may be sure the support of the Mormons will not strengthen the measure or make the Washingtonians regret their rejection of it."

Regardless of the Washington politician's opinion about suffrage for all, Utah women wasted no time in taking advantage of their newly acquired right. High on the agenda of priorities for organizations like the Relief Society was to establish a program to educate women in the area of civics, history, and political science. The Relief Society was established in 1842 by the Mormon Church and with its purpose to "prepare women for the blessings of eternal life by helping them increase their faith and personal righteousness, strengthen families and homes, and help those in need." Sarah M. Kimball, an ardent supporter of women's right to vote, set up a chapter of the Relief Society in Utah. As president of the organization there, she emphasized the need for women to become knowledgeable about how government worked and how the law operated. Kimball believed, when it came to the advancement of women, "education and agitation were the best weapons." Under her direction, many women in the Utah Territory began participating in public affairs.

Kimball was referred to by those who knew her best as the "Feminine Saint in the Field." According to the Salt Lake City correspondent for the *New York Herald*, Sister Kimball is an "apostle not whit [sic] inferior to Cady Stanton, Lucy Stone Blackwell, and other strong-minded women who figure so prominently in the columns of the newspaper as advocates of women's rights."

At a mass meeting of Mormon women held at a theater in Salt Lake City, Sister Kimball spoke to those ladies who had congregated about the importance of continuing to make their voices heard, not only to political and spiritual leaders in Utah but also in every area where women continued to be denied the right to vote or hold office.

"Sisters," Sarah Kimball began, "we have come together to express our feelings in relation to the government of the United States in which we live. We are here upon the soil of the United States. Our grandfathers fought in the Revolutionary War and many of them suffered and bled. Mine did; hence, I feel with you that I have a right to speak of the institutions of the government under which we live. We have thought much, and we have suffered much. We have been driven, outcasts almost, from the nation that gave us birth, and under whose banner we should have been protected, and inasmuch as we have conducted ourselves properly, we should have been honored. Have we transgressed any law of the United States of America? I would ask you, my sisters, have we? Then why are we here in these mountains today?

"Did we not leave the comforts and elegances of civilized and enlightened life and traverse plains? And were we not previous to that driven from place to place? And why? When we arrive at mature years the question will arise why. The immediate object of this call has been the introduction of a bill before Congress—called the Cullom Bill—which proposes to disinherit the citizens of Utah Territory, if they cling to the principles of their religion; to take from them every right of American citizens, every right that is sacred to man. And here I might say we have not come to defend women's rights, as many honorable ladies are doing throughout the United States and other countries; but we are here today to advocate man's rights—man's rights to an inheritance upon the soil of this United States territory.

"They do not allow us to be a State. Why? This bill would deprive not only our fathers, friends and sons, but it would even deprive us of the privilege of their inheritance, and from being landowners, selecting our own husbands. Against this we rebel. This is my feeling, and as far as I understand, it is the feeling of the sisters around me and before me. The object of this meeting is to give expression to our feelings. We have felt a long time, and why not express our feelings? It now becomes our duty to draft resolutions expressive of the feelings of the ladies of this city."

Kimball's speech sparked great enthusiasm among fellow suffragists. In the months to come, she and the other members of the Relief Society watched as women in the territory were admitted to the bar, placed on school boards, and served on coroner's juries.

Progress was being made, but not everyone was pleased with the advancements. Ambitious orators, office holders, and lawmakers outside Utah were frustrated that the voting women of the territory did not quickly choose to elect Gentiles who could do away with pluralistic marriage or decide to eliminate the practice on their own. When Congress realized the power of the Mormon Church was not going to be contained or subjugated by women voters as was hoped, they crafted a bill to resend the right for women to vote and abolish woman suffrage altogether. In March 1882, Congress passed an anti-polygamy act, also known as the Edmunds Act, which made it illegal for polygamists to vote, hold public office, or serve on juries. Thirteen years after the Edmunds Act was made law, Utah would be named a state, and women would once again be allowed to vote in public elections.

The time between 1882, when the Edmunds Act was approved by the House and the Senate, and 1896, when President Cleveland proclaimed Utah a state on equal footing with other states in the Union, women in the Utah Territory quietly pushed for reform. Numerous

An anti-suffrage campaign ad for Utah. Library of Congress

articles appearing in the *Salt Lake Herald* described the suffrage movement in other locations west of the Mississippi, such as Montana and Wyoming, as unqualified successes. Those stories encouraged disenfranchised women in the Utah Territory to continue fighting for their rights. They took solace in knowing that in other areas of the country suffrage was being tied to Prohibition. A woman's right to vote in Indiana would not be granted unless Prohibition was enacted. Tying the two issues together was not unlike what women in Utah were experiencing with pluralistic marriage.

Proponents for giving women the vote argued that the issues of polygamy and Prohibition should be separated, and that women suffrage should be allowed to stand alone on its merits. Harnessed to the arguments of Prohibition and polygamy made granting women the right to cast a ballot an unpopular partisan question.

Miss Phoebe Cousins, a St. Louis suffrage leader and protégé of Susan B. Anthony, applied to President Arthur to be appointed one of Utah Territory's commissioners so she could help reorganize the area and smooth the path for women to get to vote. The well-known lecturer hoped to make a difference by expressing her interests "wherever women were without a country."

Cousins was the first woman lawyer in America and the first woman to become a United States marshal. Few careers have been more romantic. A beautiful girl, she was besieged with admirers and might have made many brilliant marriages. At one time, a vice president of the United States and two United States senators sought her hand, but she disdained all offers. She had her mission to fulfill, and inexorably pursued it. She secured entrance into the law department at Washington University with some difficulty, but she graduated with honors and began her career. She made a few strong woman suffrage speeches—one at the Presbyterian Sunday school convention in Jefferson City where she startled her staid audience by asserting that "Paul's words to women amounted to nothing, for Paul was simply a crusty old bachelor with no authority to lay commands upon womankind." The other occurred at the banquet of the Mercantile Library Association, where she was toasted as "our own Phoebe Cousins." Then she spread her ambitious wings and flew away to Washington, D.C. There she received prominence and lectured before various audiences on the cause she espoused.

Ultimately the president of the United States did not appoint her a place on the seat of the Utah Commission. Cousins's actions did, however, highlight the ongoing struggles women in the territory were experiencing regarding being treated equally.

Members at the National Woman Suffrage Association reached out to Mormon and non-Mormon women in the Utah Territory to encourage them to continue fighting for the righteous cause. Women in the area had no intention of abandoning their efforts, but the division over the suffrage issue within the territory prompted them to split the movement in two. Many non-Mormon suffragists held to the belief that granting the vote to Utah women would only strengthen the political power of the Mormon Church. In 1888, Emily S. Richards, wife of Mormon Church attorney Franklin S. Richards, approached church officials with the idea of creating a Utah suffrage association. Her intention was to affiliate with the National Woman Suffrage Association, and when the proposal was approved in early 1889, the Woman Suffrage Association of Utah and leaders of the newly formed organization went to work organizing local units throughout the territory.

The first regular meeting of the Woman Suffrage Association of Utah was held on February 9, 1889, at the social hall in Salt Lake City. Mrs. Lydia D. Alder, vice president of the organization, was one of the first to address the attendees about the issue at hand. "The hand that rocks the cradle is the hand that rules the world," Mrs. Alder offered to the group. "This sentiment was written long ago; but it is just as true today as it was then. It has from time immemorial been conceded that the home (the dearest spot on Earth) is the women's kingdom. And many women are there today who desire no other sphere. History shows that down all the ages the mother who rocks the cradle and carefully raises sons has through them ruled the world.

"But shall not our daughters be taught also, and have just as many privileges as our sons? Most assuredly. We can look around us and see many of our sisters who have to struggle with the hard realities of life. Some of them chose never to marry. They own property, either much or little, on which they must pay taxes for the support of the government, both local and general. Yet they must never have a voice in the choice of government's servants. Woman suffrage is a live question before all thinking minds and many nations today. Think for a moment of the prospect confronting our own government welcoming as it does the downtrodden and oppressed of every kind to its shores. This emigration brings many who are utterly ignorant of the first true principles of government. Scheming politicians can buy this vote. . . . This has produced too much of the corruption existing today. You can see that when women everywhere gain the ballot, and we women in Utah regain our ballot, her vote, given intelligently and wisely, will offset the vote of ignorance and fraud. God speed the day."

A Utah-based newspaper titled the *Woman's Exponent* gave disenfranchised Mormon ladies of the territory, like Mrs. Alder, a voice to express their ambition to vote. *Woman's Exponent* editor and suffragist Emmeline B. Wells spoke out for the rights of women of Zion and the rights of women in all nations. "Let me explain the principles an enfranchised woman holds to," Wells wrote in an article in the November 15, 1875, edition of the *Woman's Exponent*. "She feels her political independence and that she is virtually part and parcel of the great body politic, not through her father or husband, but in her own vested right." Wells maintained that in time the skillful wording of the issues involving Mormon women would prove more effective than militant confrontations of suffragists elsewhere.

Emmeline B. Wells. Library of Congress

A wide range of women-oriented items were covered in the *Woman's Exponent*. It offered Mormon women an opportunity to refute diatribes about their religious beliefs found in other publications and included reports of their organizations and clubs as well as various social and cultural events. Articles about women's continued struggle to be given voting rights consistently appeared on the front page of the publication. An item in the "Woman Suffrage" column from the April 1, 1894, edition of the *Woman's Exponent* strongly expressed the sentiment of most women in the Utah Territory.

"To vote or not to vote!" contributor L. L. Dalton noted in her piece. "That is the question. Shall we drift with the sluggish tide in custom, and in our Organic Act rivet the fetters of perpetual minority upon the mothers of so hardy a race of men as Utah can boast?

"Shall we mar our onward progress as a Common Wealth . . . ? They can never be persuaded that you and your daughters are not equally concerned in all that pertains to this hard-won home, equal heirs to the grand estate.

"All men know it is not in us to boast; but we do not deny that our record of the past gives us room to boast of every requisite to honest, useful citizenship and we look with confidence to our husbands and fathers to see that our claims be not ignored and our rights not abridged when the crown of statehood shall rest upon the brow of our beloved Utah."

While women in the territory like Emmeline Wells continued to fight for the right to represent themselves at the polls, influential political and community leaders worked diligently on crafting a constitution to present to Congress to make Utah a state. In addition to factoring in women's rights, the matter of polygamy still had to be addressed. How to remove the main obstacle to Utah statehood while upholding a historic, religious practice presented a problem. Wilford Woodruff, president of the Mormon Church, provided a solution to the matter in 1890 when he announced he would no longer permit plural marriage in opposition to the laws of the United States. Woodruff's manifesto would prove to Washington representatives that the territory of Utah was willing to conform with the government's regulations. Agreeing to add a provision giving women equal rights would not be as clearly realized.

Mothers and wives rallied together at meetings held by the Woman Suffrage Association of Utah and made spirited speeches to persuade the public that giving women the vote needed to be tied with Utah's statehood.

"We had enjoyed the right of franchise at one time," Mrs. Zina D. H. Young told attendees at a suffrage meeting on April 11, 1889, "and yet it was taken from us. Was there any justice in this? We look for the great government of the United States and, subsequently, the great state of Utah, to again confer upon us the God-given right of suffrage, because by and with it, we will be enabled to do vast good to the world.

"Our fathers contended that 'taxation without representation' was wrong. If it were so a hundred years ago, it is no less today. There are many women in this territory who pay taxes and yet have no voice in the selection of public officers through whose hands this money is distributed."

Mrs. Ida Gibbs, another strong proponent of women's rights, echoed the sentiment. "The rights of women are entirely paramount with those of men," Mrs. Gibbs announced. "I have heard it said that woman was too good and pure to enter politics; that she would rapidly be besmeared. I do not think so. Politics cannot degrade woman, but woman can elevate and purify politics. The question of woman suffrage does not hinge upon the query as to whether the majority of women want it or not. The question simply is whether the right to vote is useful or beneficial. If it is so to man, it certainly should be to women."

More and more prominent men in the territory were joining the ranks of those in support of suffrage and continually speak in favor of suffrage. Hon. W. H. King, attorney and Latter Day Saints missionary, and member of the House of Representatives, and Hon. John T. Caine, delegate

Sitting like an island in the middle of the Intermountain West, the Utah Territory, founded by emigrants seeking a refuge for their religious beliefs, was an anomaly among the western territories that started becoming states after the Civil War. Mostly traveling on foot, sometimes pushing handcarts from Missouri to the Salt Lake Valley, about sixty thousand Mormon emigrants—members of the Church of Jesus Christ of Latter Day Saints, which had been founded in New York in 1830, had carved out a home in the wilderness based on their own beliefs, arriving there between about 1847 and 1868.

The territory they settled would become part of the United States shortly after the first pioneers—who called themselves "Saints"—arrived. Formerly claimed by Mexico, the land would be ceded to the United States after the Mexican-American War. Interestingly, even having left persecution in the United States behind, many leaders of the church actually believed that, after all, the best way to preserve freedom of religion for the people of the Mormon faith was to seek status as a fully fledged state with its own political structure.

Starting in 1849, the citizens of what would become the Utah Territory began petitioning the U.S. government for statehood under the name Deseret. Initially, the request was denied for several reasons, including the large physical size of the territory (which included much more land than the current state of Utah), the small size of the population, and the ongoing struggles over slavery in the United States However, the petition got the ball rolling, and in 1850, Congress created Utah Territory—a smaller slice of the original proposal—as a stepping stone to statehood.

For the next fifty years, Utah Territory would continue to submit statehood petitions to the U.S. government, but even after the Civil War settled issues of slavery, one issue stood out as a barrier to Utah joining the union as a political entity with full states' rights.

Federal law forbade the practice of polygamy, which was at that time an important part of Mormon culture and religion.

In 1870, in one of the more ironic moments in western history, Utah Territory granted women the right to vote in the territorial constitution. The move was widely supported by Mormon leaders and non-Mormons in the territory, alike, but for opposing reasons. Church leader Brigham Young believed that if women in Utah territory had the right to vote, the practice of polygamy would be seen as less oppressive to women. Non-Mormons thought that women, if given the option, would vote to end the institution.

With statehood in the balance, in the 1880s, pressure was put on the church—and effectively therefore the territory—to end polygamy. One pressure point was the 1887 Edmunds-Tucker Act, which revoked Utah women's right to vote, granted by the territorial constitution. The issue was eventually resolved in 1890 when then church president Wilford Woodruff disavowed the practice of plural marriage as a tenet of Mormonism, finally making it possible for the long-hoped-for admission as a state in 1896. And the right to vote for women was part of that statehood—the second state to include it as part of their constitution.

to the United States House of Representatives both attended the suffrage convention held at the assembly hall in Salt Lake in October 1889. "I am in sympathy with the movement," King announced to the attendees at the event. "I cannot conceive that man is superior to woman. Woman educates, trains and instills principles of patriotism in the minds of the youth, and by doing so she accomplishes a great deal of good."

Representative Caine echoed his colleague's assessment and added that "depriving the women of Utah of the right to vote was an outrage, as they all voted in a commendable manner, although it has charged that they vote as cattle do; but it is not so. It is only a question of time when women will get their rights," Caine continued. "I sustain with my whole heart the movement with this organization. Equal rights at the ballot-box will sweep evil from our midst."

Those opposed to woman suffrage were encouraged by articles that appeared in newspapers which noted that giving women the right to vote in Wyoming did not have the impact initially touted by the women's movement. According to the March 7, 1890, edition of the *Salt Lake Herald*, "Woman suffrage in Wyoming has been neither a gratifying success nor a disgraceful failure. Such effect as it has had in the community has been good, but the effect has been slight and is growing less and less every year. The truth is, the novelty having worn off the women, as a class, are not half as interested in the ballot as they were before they were allowed to 'enjoy' it. The great majority of the Wyoming women do not go to the polls or take part in elections, except at times when there are local contests involving questions with which the immediate neighborhood is concerned."

An article in the January 20, 1891, edition of *The Utopian* maintained that if the right to vote was granted to women in Utah Territory, her life would not be easier nor would her labor be lighter. The article argued that women should concentrate on delivering to her state "a half a dozen manly voices through motherhood who could grow up to be informed voters."

"Whenever a woman enters the political arena, she sacrifices that charm of womanhood, delicacy of manner, which cannot be kept pure under the coarser contaminating influences," *The Utopian* article noted. "We do not assert that politics is degrading to women, but we do think it does not elevate; neither do we think women wield the purifying influence at the polls suffrage advocates claim. We have not observed a case in years of observation where the voice of woman is felt in the primaries, the conventions or as representatives, either municipal or executive, though a single female delegate to a county convention may be an exception. The better class of women care little for the ballot or political honors, feeling that 'the hand that rocks the cradle rules the world,' that the mother who gives to her state is sufficient. . . .

"The true woman who would make the most of her every God-given attribute asks not for the ballot, but for love and home, where the carols of babyhood are sung to the sweetest of babies, where home is heaven and where the weary husband may find rest and aching hearts sympathy."

The Woman Suffrage Association of Utah campaigned relentlessly against such archaic beliefs, vigorously encouraging everyone to attend her regular meetings. Suffragists maintained that the public needed to know how crucial it was that women have the right to choose a life for themselves that reflected their own ideals and leaders that would represent their values.

The state constitutional convention held in Salt Lake from March 4 to May 8, 1895, proved to be a major turning point for woman suffrage. All the years of holding meetings and rallies to petition for voting rights was about to pay off. A last-ditch effort from Mormon traditionalists to stop any bill granting women suffrage got underway on March 29, 1895. Mormon scholar B. H. Roberts spent two hours explaining why woman suffrage was a bad idea. He laid down the rule that suffrage should be granted only to those who could act independently and without dictation. He spoke out against any woman over twenty-one years of age being allowed to vote. Roberts maintained that married women could not act independently.

"By all the laws of nature, spoken through the words of God, man is the head of the woman," the scholar stated. "I do not believe that this headship means tyranny and oppression. Woman was not taken from the head of man for fear she might rule over him, but from under his arm that he might protect her, such is the natural rule.

"But is the suffrage based on mental equality? Were the slaves enfranchised because of mental equality? No. It was to give them protection against their former masters. The franchise has always been given as a matter of protection. Do our wives, mothers, sisters and daughters need protection against us?

"Now, gentlemen . . . look at the effect of this in the family. Shall we not leave some refuge for man in this world, where he can come out of the strife and bitterness that is oft engendered in business professionals and political life. I call on you as men forming a new state constitution, beware how you deal with this question and lay not the foundation for wrecking domestic peace. Leave men, I say, some asylum, some refuge, from the storms and cares of life. Do this and then, through plot and counterplot, through gain and loss, through glory and disgrace, along the plains where discord rears eternal babel, the gentle stream of human happiness may glide on. I pray you go back to caucus, think this question over, do right as it is in your hearts and as God gives you the light to see it."

Mr. B. H. Roberts's assessment of woman suffrage was shared only by a small few. The preponderance of delegates at the convention wanted statehood and were keenly aware that those they represented wanted a provision granting women the right to vote included in the constitution being drafted. On March 31, 1895, Roberts was asked to resign if he could not refrain from speaking against woman suffrage. He refused to change his course.

Delegations in favor of granting women voting rights boldly told their cohorts the success of the woman's movement was a foregone conclusion.

Women had fought long and hard to gain suffrage, and they had proven through independent surveys that constituents want them to have it.

Political leaders attending the constitutional convention agreed to add woman suffrage to the constitution on April 5, 1895. More than 250 citizens of Salt Lake submitted letters to various delegates expressing their disapproval and pledged to vote against the constitution if woman suffrage was included. A few men who didn't want women to get the vote but approved suffrage being added to the constitution because they wanted their wives home instead of fighting voting rights made their feelings known. They sent letters and poems that expressed their sentiments to politicians. One read as follows:

> Oh mother, please, mother, come home with me now. The afternoon is slipping by fast. You said you were coming right home from the polls as soon as your ballot was cast. Poor father came in for his dinner at noon and not a mouthful he could find. And the words that he said as he slammed the front door left a strong smell of sulphur behind.

Those in favor of giving women the vote far outweighed the naysayers. Representatives from suffrage groups across the West stood outside the convention hall giving impromptu speeches and outlining the reasons why the time had come for women in Utah to be allowed to vote.

On April 18, 1895, delegates at the state's constitutional convention voted in favor of woman suffrage. In the final analysis, no argument against giving women the right to vote could be sustained. After fighting for more than twenty-five years, woman suffrage had become law in Utah. Women would once more vote in Utah. Newspaper editor Emmeline Wells was the first to send the good news to Susan B. Anthony. Anthony responded with sincere congratulations to all the women in the new state. "Hurrah for Utah," her telegram read. "Number three state that establishes a genuine form of government."

CHAPTER FIVE

─ ●●─ ──

Becoming Citizens:
Woman's Suffrage in California

*I take it America never gave any better principle to the world
than the safety of letting every human being have the power of
protection in its own hands. I claim it for woman. The moment
she has the ballot, I shall think the cause is won.*
—WENDELL PHILLIPS, AMERICAN ABOLITIONIST, ADVOCATE FOR
NATIVE AMERICANS, ORATOR, AND ATTORNEY

When suffragist Susan B. Anthony boarded the passenger car of
the Union Pacific Railroad in Ogden, Utah, in late December
1871, the train was filled to capacity. Men, women, children, livestock,
baggage, and crates containing food and supplies were being loaded onto
the vehicle bound for Chicago. Weary and carrying an oversized satchel
bulging with clothing, books, and papers, the fifty-one-year-old woman
climbed aboard and began the slow procession past the throngs of people occupying various seats and berths. She snaked her way toward the
semi-private compartments until she found the one she was to occupy
for the duration of the trip. The pair Anthony would be traveling East
with had already arrived and made themselves comfortable. She smiled
at the congenial-looking couple as she entered. California congressman
Aaron A. Sargent politely got to his feet to help her stow away her bag.

He introduced himself, then introduced his accomplished wife, Ellen, to Anthony, who returned the kindness.

Not long after Anthony was settled, Ellen admitted to being familiar with her work. Anthony's crusade to acquire the right to vote for women had been covered in the Sacramento newspapers as well as the publications in Nevada City, California, where the politician and his family lived. She had joined the fight for woman's suffrage in 1852. Since that time, she had traveled from town to town, inspiring women to fight for equal rights. The crusade, which initially began in Seneca Falls in New York in 1840, had expanded westward. Once Wyoming granted women the privilege to cast their ballots, suffrage rose up in territories beyond the Mississippi to battle for the opportunity to do the same. Crusaders reasoned if women could gain that right state by state the federal government would be persuaded to pass an amendment making it law.

From June to December of 1871, Anthony had traveled more than thirteen thousand miles, delivered 108 lectures, and attended close to two hundred rallies on the issue of woman's suffrage. There were others such as Emily Pitts Stevens, who helped form the California Woman Suffrage Association, and physician and minister Anna Howard Shaw who had joined the fight and were hosting meetings to inform and educate women about the movement. It was essential that the message of equality be heard in every mining community, fishing village, and major city from San Francisco to Los Angeles. Women needed to be encouraged to petition for enfranchisement. They needed to be reminded they were entitled to speak for themselves and stand against fathers and husbands voting for them. Anthony and the other dedicated suffragists had been able to share the message with women in Kansas, Wyoming, Utah, Washington, and Oregon; they had great hope the ladies in California would back reform.

Anthony couldn't have found a more receptive audience for her message than Congressman Sargent and his wife. Ellen had founded the first suffrage group in Nevada City, California, in 1869, and Aaron was in full support of giving women the vote. The Sargents had moved to California from Massachusetts in 1849 and settled in Nevada City in 1850. In addition to owning and operating the newspaper the *Nevada Daily Journal*, Aaron was an attorney and former U. S. senator. Ellen was a homemaker and mother who was active in the Methodist Church. She firmly believed that women could not attain their highest development until they "had the same large opportunities and the same large chances as her brothers have."

The journey East would prove to be particularly slow. Several feet of snow covered the tracks, and the train took longer to reach its destination. The Sargents generously shared the food and tea they had brought with Anthony. According to Susan, the kindness the pair showed her made the trip enjoyable. "Mr. Sargent made the tea, unpacked the hampers, and served as general steward," she wrote in her journal on December 29, 1871. "He drew the line at washing dishes."

Between Ogden, Utah, and Bittercreek, Wyoming, the trio discussed the influence women such as Laura de Force Gordon were having on the movement. Gordon was a law student and prominent suffragist. She had delivered the first suffrage speech in California in February 1868. She proposed that the constitutions of several states should be amended "so that white and black, red and yellow, of both sexes, can exercise their civil rights."

It was Gordon who helped bring together suffrage society members scattered throughout Northern California. At her urging, on January 24, 1870, dedicated women congregated in San Francisco to discuss the movement and learn what needed to be done to pave the way for the vote. Gordon delivered a powerful speech which inspired even the most retiring ladies to make their voices heard. She and her physician husband had moved from the East Coast in 1867. Her early influences on the issue of women's suffrage were Elizabeth Cady Stanton and Susan B. Anthony. She was a powerful speaker and greatly admired by Ellen and Aaron Sargent.

Ida Husted Harper

In May 1887, author and woman suffrage leader Ida Husted Harper wrote, "Men have two ways of righting their wrongs, by force and by ballot. Both are denied to women, one by nature the other by men." Born in Fairfield, Indiana, in 1851, Ida's controversial ideas appeared in a regular column she penned in the firefighter's union publication, *Fireman's Magazine*.

Ida's college career began at the University of Indiana and ended when she graduated from Stanford University in 1895. She served as an editor for the *New York Sunday Sun* and *Harper's Bazaar*. She had been a proponent for women's rights since her high school years, and her quest to help secure suffrage was further enhanced when she met Susan B. Anthony in 1878. The two women became close friends, and Ida would go on to write a three-volume biography about Anthony, entitled *The Life and Work of Susan B. Anthony*. She would later coauthor the book *The History of Woman Suffrage* with Anthony.

Ida Husted Harper. Library of Congress

In addition to the numerous articles and books on woman suffrage, Ida served as a delegate and speaker from the International Council of Women and the International Woman Suffrage Alliance. In 1917, Ida accepted a position in Washington, D.C., as head of the Leslie Bureau of Suffrage Education. The bureau's purpose was to promote the cause through a greater visibility in the public eye. It was believed that Ida could bring great attention to the movement through her writings. Indeed, the steady stream of letters, articles, and pamphlets issued from her office played a large role in the successful campaign for passage of the Nineteenth Amendment.

Ida's final literary work was the contribution of articles on woman suffrage and suffrage biographies to the fourteenth edition of the *Encyclopedia Britannica*. She died on March 14, 1931, on almost the exact anniversary of Susan B. Anthony's death of March 13, 1906. Ida was eighty years old when she died at her home in Washington, D.C.

Despite the problems the weather posed for the eastbound Union Pacific Railroad passengers, Anthony and the Sargents filled every moment with conversation about what should be included in everyone's natural rights. On the morning of January 1, 1872, Anthony, the Sargents, and J. H. Hayford, editor of the *Laramie Sentinel*, were sharing breakfast when Susan, Ellen, and Aaron learned of a bill to repeal the woman's suffrage law in Wyoming. "The law had been passed by a Democratic legislature as a jest," Anthony wrote in her journal, "but five Democrats voted for repeal and four Republicans against it. Governor Campbell, a Republican, vetoed this repeal bill and woman's suffrage still stands, as a territorial legislature cannot pass a bill over a governor's veto." The suffragists breathed a sigh of relief regarding the veto. If such a thing were to have happened, the push for women's right to vote in California would have taken a serious hit. "Here we are at noon, stuck in snowdrifts five miles west of Sherman, on a steep grade, with one hundred men shoveling in front of us," Anthony added in her journal entry. "Dined, Mr. Sargent officiating, on roast turkey, jelly, bread and butter, spice cake and excellent tea. At dark, wind and snow blowing terrifically, but a bright sky. The conversation about how to advance the cause continues on."

One of the elements about the suffragists' movements in California of sincere concern to Anthony and the Sargents was that the women's groups had split into two factions. Elizabeth Cady Stanton and Susan B. Anthony were linked to the radical sect of the movement. Recognized as the conservatives were two of the founders of the American Woman Suffrage Association, Henry Blackwell and his wife, orator and suffragist Lucy Stone. Both were able to recruit members to the cause, but it was important that they be viewed as a unified front and not two separate entities with different goals. Those against giving women the vote accused the radical suffragists of being socialists and supporting spiritualism and free love. That kind of false labeling threatened to undermine the basis for the movement.

As January 2, 1872, came into view, Anthony and the Sargents explored ways to unify the two movements in California. The train was still stationary, and the railroad company had supplied the passengers with dried fish and crackers. According to Anthony's journal, she and the Sargents tabled their discussion about the suffrage movement long enough to serve tea to the nursing mothers on the train.

"Five days out from Ogden!" Anthony wrote. "This is indeed a fearful ordeal, fastened here in a snowbank, midway of the continent at the top of the mountains. They are melting snow for the boilers and for drinking water. A train loaded with coal is behind us, so there is no danger of our suffering from cold. . . . Here, we remained all night and, with the verified air and the smoke from the engine, were almost suffocated, while the wind blew so furiously we could not venture to open the doors which was fine. Inside we continued to pontificate on the issue at hand and the future of the vote in California."

Among the issues Anthony and the Sargents discussed was the movement's rising stars. San Jose, California, resident Sarah Louise Knox Goodrich was one of those stars. Knox Goodrich was a wealthy and politically well-connected woman. She had a great deal of influence over her late husband, William J. Knox, a physician and political leader who held women in high regard and believed they should be given the same consideration in many respects as men. While senator of the Santa Clara County area, William J. Knox secured a bill aiding married women's property. In 1874, his wife successfully petitioned the California State Legislature to pass a law that would allow women to hold educational offices such as school boards.

Four years later another force to reckon with in the suffragists' movement lobbied the state legislature for the Woman Lawyer's Bill. In 1878, Laura de Force Gordon and Clara Shortridge Foltz drafted changes to the bill, which read that a "white male" may practice law, to read instead that a "person" may practice law.

Los Angeles suffragist Elizabeth Anne Kingsbury formed a woman suffrage association in 1883 and traveled about the state to recruit women to the movement who believed securing the vote was essential. There were many more women crusaders who had humble beginnings in similar suffrage organizations throughout the state. All contributed their share to the advancement of women's right to vote. They stood on the shoulders of the early leaders Susan B. Anthony and Ellen Clark Sargent.

By the time the Sargents and Anthony arrived in Washington, D.C., on January 10, 1872, the trio had thoroughly reviewed the Fourteenth and Fifteenth Amendments, and Susan and Ellen had decided the wording in the amendments made it clear that women were already enfranchised. The Fourteenth Amendment affirmed the rights of freed women and men in 1868. The law stated that everyone born in the United States, including former slaves, was an American citizen. The Fifteenth Amendment affirmed that the right to vote "shall not be denied on account of race." Aaron Sargent pointed out that the amendment specified equality for male slaves and that female slaves were excluded as were all women, regardless of race. Aaron maintained that a new amendment would have to be drafted to secure rights for women. Anthony insisted that women should be challenged to vote based on verbiage in the Fourteenth and Fifteenth Amendments. Aaron respected her dedication and pointed out the problems inherent with voting "illegally." During the long train trip, he had already begun working on the text for a new amendment. His early draft consisted of just twenty-eight words. "The right of citizens of the United States to vote shall not be denied or abridged by the United States or by any state on account of sex." When the time was right, Aaron planned to introduce the text as an amendment.

By the time the Sargents and Anthony parted company in Washington, D.C., they had forged a lasting friendship. Over the next twenty years the three would make tremendous strides in the fight to gain the right to vote for women. Anthony would travel throughout the country promoting the suffrage movement. Aaron would go back and forth from California to the Capitol, and Ellen would focus her efforts on the northern portion of California. Their progress would be marked in the letters they would exchange.

Anthony wrote the Sargents in early April 1872 to share that she was soliciting lecturers and organizers to be present at the next convention held in Washington. "We need to decide upon the best methods of presenting our principles and policies in the different states," she noted. "At that point we shall be able to recommend to you of California the right woman who can organize all the suffragists into one force. It does seem a very great pity to pay the traveling expenses of anybody to go over to California to organize when you have lots of splendid women who could go out and do it for you just as well as anybody imported into the state."

Anthony, the Sargents, and several suffrage leaders in California felt the interest in the cause was in danger of waning. Many of the women were turning their focus from suffrage to temperance work. For some dedicated crusaders, the Woman's Christian Temperance Union (WCTU) movement was problematic. The agenda for the WCTU was less about women's citizenship and more about spreading the word that alcohol was a destructive force. Conservative suffragists believed the anti-alcohol message and that a woman's right to vote were equally as important. Radical supporters of women's enfranchisement were fearful of never acquiring the vote if it was synonymous with Prohibition. Regardless of the possible misperceptions, members of the National Woman Suffrage Association aligned themselves with the growing number of WCTU members with the goal of promoting women's issues.

In November 1873, Ellen Sargent sent a letter to Anthony expressing her continued enthusiasm for advancing the cause in California through those affiliated with the WCTU. "I cannot help but reflect on the thousands of women with tender consciences that believe they have a duty not to be shirked, to represent themselves in the affairs of government,"

Ellen wrote. "Take heart. Women in California know votes talk, votes count, votes command respect."

Aaron Sargent's letter to Anthony in early 1874 further expressed how devoted he and his wife were to women in California gaining enfranchisement. "During the political campaign, before an immense audience in San Francisco I addressed the audience in the following manner. 'Ladies and gentlemen, fellow citizens. I trust the time is near at hand when the phrase "fellow citizens" will not need the explanatory remark. Ladies and gentlemen, I trust we are nearing the day when our wives and daughters will share with us the duties and privilege of citizenship, and give expression to their principles and views at the ballot box. I am in favor of this great reform and hail the day when it shall purify politics by the influence of women, exerted directly and legitimately at elections.'"

In the fall of 1875, the California Woman Suffrage Association was holding regular meetings throughout the state and encouraging members to get out the message to the public at large that women deserved the right to vote. The September 21, 1875, edition of the *Los Angeles Herald* reported on the efforts of the organization and how the suggested changes were being received by some of the opposite sex. "Men shudder at the violent innovations in the autonomy of government, and vigorously oppose great changes in the social system," the article read. "Not among the least important question which has agitated the minds of the great thinkers of the present century is the social status of women. In the progress of human events, she has emerged from the condition of a slave nearly to that of an equal, but the final step, the complete emancipation of the sex and her elevation to an equal share of the government is far from being accomplished, and, in fact, is so heartily opposed by the great majority of mankind, even in the New World, that the weakest demagogues have scarcely considered it worth the advocacy."

Although women were decades away from gaining the vote, the message the suffragists carried in newspapers, flyers, and speeches was having an impact as it made its way across the state. The influence of crusaders' cries could be measured by the victories at the state legislative level. After law student Clara Shortridge Foltz and fellow suffragist Laura de Force Gordon managed to get the Woman Lawyer's Bill passed, Clara became the first woman lawyer on the West Coast of the United States. Women were now allowed to argue a case before a jury, but because they were not allowed to vote, they were not allowed to serve on a jury.

Congressman Aaron Sargent. Library of Congress

Suffragents

In 1911, actress, playwright, and "suffragette" Vida Sutton coined the term "suffragent." A suffragent referred to a man who was big enough to see that women should be given the right to vote. "This type of man is one of the most powerful allies of the cause of women," Vida explained to a reporter for the *New York Times*. "He not only does not hinder but does all that he can to help."

From the time the woman suffrage movement was first launched in 1846, there were many prominent suffragents who played significant roles in helping women secure the right to vote.

At the urging of Elizabeth Cady Stanton, California senator Aaron Augustus Sargent introduced the first federal woman suffrage amendment in 1878. The amendment was reintroduced in every succeeding Congress until adopted in 1920. "I believe the time is rapidly coming when all men will conclude that it is no longer wise or judicious to exclude one half of the intelligence and more than one half of the virtue of the people from the ballot box," Sargent remarked in April 1878.

A male supporter of woman's suffrage, 1913. Library of Congress

San Francisco mayor Adolph Sutro echoed those sentiments in March 1896. "I believe equality is the basic principle of our government—hence women should assume all the responsibilities that arise out of her moral and mental endowments as a citizen," Sutro told the *San Francisco Chronicle*. "Woman's advent as a voter will be the means through which the government may be perpetuated, as embodying justice, equality, and righteousness."

Frederick Douglass, American abolitionist, orator and lecturer, was present at the Seneca Falls Women's Rights Convention of 1848 and advocated for women's rights along with abolition and the rights of African Americans. At a meeting of the National Council of Women in 1895, he reminded an enthusiastic crowd of what he had written about the issue in 1848. "A discussion of the rights of animals would be regarded with far more complacency by many of what are called the wise and the good of our land than would be a discussion of the rights of women. . . . We hold women to be justly entitled to all we claim for man."

In Utah, businessman and senator Reed Smoot introduced on the floor of Congress in 1919 petitions from women in his state for national suffrage to be approved. Utah women's right to vote had been restored in 1895. "Giving women the vote," Senator Smoot explained to fellow officeholders, "has made no daughter less beautiful, no wife less devoted, no mother less inspiring." Theodore Roosevelt and members of his Bull Moose Party were proponents of women's right to vote. In 1912, the future president spoke out in favor of woman suffrage and became one of the cause's greatest supporters. While a senior at Harvard in 1880, Roosevelt wrote a paper advocating equal rights for women, including the fact that they shouldn't change their names when they got married. "Working women have the same need to protection that working men have," he announced in a speech he gave at the National Convention of the Progressive Party in August 1912. "The ballot is as necessary for one class as to the other; we do not believe that with the two sexes there is identity of function; but we do believe there should be equality of right."

In addition to the numerous public figures who could count themselves as suffragents, there were average men about town and home who were included in the mix. An article in the May 10, 1915, edition of the *Pittsburgh Post-Gazette* is testament to how some men subtly became part of the movement.

"I got to thinking tonight, after I had cooked the supper, and washed the dishes, and put the boys to bed and shaved (because I don't have time to shave in the morning since I have to be at the

An early illustration showing men's support for woman suffrage. Library of Congress

office by 8). I got to thinking about old Pepys, the Englishman, who kept a diary in which he put down things he was afraid to say out loud and didn't want anybody to know, just as a sort of relief to his feelings. And I couldn't help wondering whether Mrs. Pepys wasn't a good deal like my Maria, so blamed eager to be 'emancipated' that she has to make a slave of her husband.

"Now that's a pretty strong thing to say, and I wouldn't go around saying it, or anyway where Maria could hear me, but I can write it, just as old Pepys did, and it certainly makes a fellow feel better to get such rankling thoughts out of his system by putting them on paper.

"Maria has always been addicted to talking in her sleep. So one night when I heard her muttering something that sounded like 'votes for women' and 'taxation without representation.' I didn't think much of it but turned over and went asleep again myself.

"But the next evening I must confess I got somewhat of a shock. I was coming home I remember. I had just got off the 5:52 train at the Crafton station, and right at the corner of our street where the big billboards are was a big sign reading: Votes for Women! Mrs. Pankhurst, the Famous Suffragette, Will Lecture at the Auditorium Thursday Evening. Subject, 'Rouse, Ye Slaves!' Chairwoman of the Meeting, Mrs. Maria Tompkins.

"I read that last line over six times and even then I didn't understand it. Not that I doubted Maria's ability to preside over any gathering that ever assembled from the Woman's Foreign Missionary Society down to the United States Senate, but I had never heard her say anything about joining the suffragists, and she is not characteristically reticent. Not in the least.

"Although at the time my arms were full of packages I had brought out from town at Maria's request, including a portable vacuum cleaner, two dozen Florida oranges, Johnny's old roller skates which had been repaired, and a pound and a half of lean rib lamb chops I started running and never stopped until I arrived at the front door of our house.

"Maria let me in, and although trembling inwardly, I thought it best to treat the matter facetiously.

"'Good evening, Mrs. Chairwoman,' I began when Maria interrupted me in a most disconcerting manner.

"'The gentleman is out of order,' she said. 'This is not the time to discuss unfinished business. How did you come to forget that package of dress goods at Brown and Thompson's and the pair of rubbers I told you to get for Johnny at Shuman's? I see they aren't here.'

"'Well, I got the oranges first,' I started to explain, when Maria cut me real short again.

"'I see you did. Well, I'll entertain a motion to lay them on the table, and now come on in to supper for everything's getting cold. You're 20 minutes late and this meeting is adjourned.'"

By 1881, Ellen and Aaron A. Sargent were spending more time in California meeting with various women's clubs and encouraging them to not grow weary in fighting for women's rights. The Sargents moved from Nevada City, California, to San Francisco. Aaron opened a law office, and Ellen organized the city's first women's club, called The Century Club. The Century Club was dedicated to raising public awareness of the woman suffrage campaign. No matter how busy they were, Ellen and Aaron routinely exchanged letters with Anthony, who was making her way through the midsection of the country delivering speeches about the cause to suffrage associations. On February 27, 1881, Anthony wrote Ellen about spending time with fellow activists Laura de Force Gordon and style reformer Amelia Jenks Bloomer. Bloomer represented advocates in Iowa, and Gordon, a member of the National American Woman Suffrage Association, had spent a great deal of time in California gathering together fellow believers who were fighting for citizenship.

"How pleased I am to know that Mr. Sargent will continue to introduce a bill granting women the opportunity to vote," Anthony shared with Ellen. "By the way, a newspaper man in Washington whispered into my ears, as a dead secret, that Senator Sargent was to be a part of [President] Garfield's cabinet and such a rejoicing we had. What good news for the cause! While the Senator is ever and ever so much to us—he without his wife wouldn't be but the half—would he?"

Any hope that President Garfield would appoint Aaron Sargent to his cabinet and, therefore, be of further help to the suffrage cause was dashed when Garfield was assassinated in September 1881. Aaron was appointed ambassador to Germany by President Chester A. Arthur. The Sargents moved to Berlin where Aaron served as ambassador for two years. All the while, Anthony and the Sargents corresponded. Anthony kept the couple abreast of the fight for suffrage. One of the items she sent them to show the progress being made for the cause was an article from the July 7, 1882, edition of the *Petaluma Weekly*.

The reporter for the California newspaper asked Anthony what she had accomplished with her work for woman suffrage. "Well, I should say we had accomplished a great deal," Anthony responded. "Since the beginning of the woman suffrage agitation thirty years ago we have gained school suffrage in twelve states; law, theology and medicine, all the professions have been thrown open to us; all the western colleges and seminaries admit women; there are in this country 1,000 licensed female doctors; there are fifty female lawyers, and women are allowed to practice in the Supreme Court of the United States, although a number of states still shut us out; there are forty female ministers in the Universalist church alone, while hundreds of licensed female ministries are in the Methodist church doing the best kind of revival work. Thirty years ago, women could only cook, sew and teach. Now, not a trade hardly but has women in it. Women are managers of large stores and businesses and manage great farms with success. Why, the largest farm in one county in Illinois is owned and managed by a woman. Eastern people ought to go West and see how women are getting along with only a few of their rights."

Women's suffrage conventions, such as the one that took place in Omaha, Nebraska, in late September 1882, were routinely held, and advocates across the country flocked to the events. Many influential ladies from California made the trip to learn what advancements were being made and to get reinvigorated by the speeches delivered by Elizabeth Cady Stanton and Lucy Stone. In Anthony's view, the worthy struggle had produced important results. No one involved with the fight for the vote believed the change would happen quickly. It was incumbent upon the leaders of the women's organizations to keep advocates charged and committed to the long battle. In a letter written to Anthony from Ellen Sargent in July 1884 upon her return to the states after two years in Germany, she expressed her concern that the country's suffragists were losing faith in the cause.

"Watch woman!" Ellen refers to Miss Anthony. "How is it with our country's women? Have we any influence in shaping the legislation of this country? Have we any power hidden or acknowledged? In short have women anything to do with this present campaign? Will anybody do anything for us? Will we do anything for ourselves? A man told me last week that the woman's suffrage question in the country was about dead. That there are really only a handful of the people who care anything at all about it; that it makes scarcely a ripple in the affairs of the world. Of course, I dissented entirely from viewing things from his standpoint as he never did believe in equal rights for women and never will."

Anthony assured Ellen that advocates were "reaping the harvest from all the long years of work" and that "more and more women are coming together, speaking ably for themselves, and are devoted to the cause." That statement not only referred to how women were coming together in the East but west of the Mississippi, too, chiefly in California.

Women were making major advancements in California. Many were being elected to school boards and hospital boards. They were assuming key positions in the labor market and insisting on equal wages for equal work. Just as more women were becoming involved in the quest for statewide enfranchisement, the suffrage movement experienced a tragic loss. On August 14, 1887, Aaron Sargent passed away in his home in San Francisco. He had been struggling with his health for more than a year prior to his death. He died from complications of an old malarial fever. He had never ceased to be a strong proponent for women's rights and had consistently spoken out for women's right to vote while serving in political office. His absence would be keenly felt by the National American Woman Suffrage Association.

Ellen Clark Sargent and her daughter honored Senator Sargent's memory by dedicating themselves completely to the suffrage movement. Ellen accepted the position of treasurer of the NAWSA and represented California at the women's convention in Washington in early 1888. She delivered speeches alongside other suffrage leaders such as Laura de Force Gordon and Abigail Scott Duniway. "I'm as earnest as ever for the vote," Ellen assured Susan Anthony in a letter dated December 5, 1889. Anthony echoed the sentiment in her return correspondence and embarked on a trip through South Dakota, Wyoming, Colorado, and Kansas to rally advocates around the enfranchisement issue.

Ellen remained in California and, in 1896, was meeting with a growing band of women in the state demanding the enfranchisement of their gender. She was hopeful that the aggressive manner in which the unified women were working would result in an amendment giving women the vote to be introduced in the November election. Ellen, Susan, and other leaders of the movement believed winning in California was crucial to that cause. They reasoned that if California gave women the right to vote, the reluctant, conservative East would follow suit.

The California Woman Suffrage Amendment, also known as Amendment 6, was placed on the ballot of November 3, 1896.

Despite the great strides suffragists had made in California, there was a major hurdle with which they continued to struggle to overcome. Anti-suffrage activists could not or would not separate women wanting the right to vote from Prohibition. Somehow those two issues were intertwined. Weeks prior to the state legislature's scheduled review of the amendment that would give women the vote, the Liquor Dealers League aggressively intervened. League officials launched an appeal to saloon owners, hotel proprietors, druggists, and grocers, urging them to defeat the motion. Anti-activists also petitioned Chinese male citizens to vote against such a bill. The Chinese men disliked the idea of self-governing women and were easily convinced the measure would give women so much freedom their culture would be threatened. The tactics worked.

The California Woman Suffrage Amendment was defeated. The amendment prevailed in the southern portion of the state and in the mining regions of the Sierra Nevada Mountains. The amendment received eighty thousand votes in favor while ninety-five thousand were cast against it. Ellen believed that with continued hard work, those that voted against could be won over. Although it was a disappointment to the advocates of the proposition, there was reason to be encouraged.

In June 1901, newspapers across the country reported on the actions of both Susan Anthony and Ellen Sargent in their quest to keep suffrage at the forefront of the population's thoughts. According to the June 13, 1901, edition of *Ottawa Daily Republic*, Anthony informed suffragists at a session of the NAWSA in Washington, D.C., that the leaders of the American Federation of Labor were supportive of the cause. After Anthony spoke to the federation, the chairman of the revolution let her know that the organization's president and secretary would support an amendment giving women the vote.

Meanwhile in California, Ellen had filed suit against the supervisors of San Francisco County for collecting taxes from her but not giving her the right to vote on anything for which she was paying taxes. Her defiant act prompted women who felt the same outrage to join the suffrage movement. The Northern California suffrage groups saw a substantial increase in membership. Advocates participated in public marches, made mass appearances at county fairs delivering impromptu speeches, and joined city parades to spread the word that "without the vote, women had no hope."

Just before every annual convention the California Woman Suffrage Association held between 1902 and 1909, organization leaders met with leaders of the legislature to advocate that women be allowed to exercise the right of suffrage. Each time they respectfully requested that Amendment 6 be reintroduced, Ellen Clark Sargent, now honorary president of the California Equal Suffrage Association, challenged women to educate themselves about how government worked. She wanted followers to be informed citizens once the right to vote was granted.

"ALL TOGETHER NOW! STOP HER!"

All together now! Stop Her! Library of Congress

"We must step out into the open and make ourselves so well acquainted with government in all its bearings that we will be considered an authority upon the points we shall have investigated and thus command the respect of the most intelligent people, men and women," Ellen Clark Sargent told suffragists at the 1909 convention. "Our watchword should be duty—not what we individually want, but what will be for the general good. Victor Hugo has well expressed this sentiment in his admirable book *Les Miserables*—I quote: 'It is a terrible thing to be happy! How content one is! How all sufficient one finds it! How being in possession of the false object of life, one forgets the true object, duty!'

"This idea will save us from the pettiness of selfishness and induct us into the true largeness of living. Not to think only or mostly of ourselves, and how matters affect us individually, but how they may affect the larger outside world—the majority. This would make us truly but a 'little lower than the angels.' ... Speaking with and for women of the present day with whom we hold new and dearer relations than ever before in these glad days of our emancipation from the restricted duties of the past, we look about for a new way in which to express our surplus energy. We have a duty to replace the old and worn out systems of the past."

Inspired by Sargent's words, suffragists from Humboldt to Happy Valley held rallies, participated in parades, and even went door-to-door in some cities to explain the importance of allowing women to vote. By early 1911, advocates managed to gain enough support for enfranchisement that political leaders committed to placing the amendment on the ballot. Senate Constitutional Amendment 4, sponsored by Republican state senator Charles W. Bell from Pasadena and granting women the right to vote in California, would be considered in a special election held on October 10, 1911.

Editorials and opinion pieces against woman suffrage appeared in the *Los Angeles Times* between January and October of 1911. Many Democratic congressmen and legislators opposed the amendment and cited as their reasons that women were too weak to take on such responsibility. "Women are incapable of physically dominating men," an article from the January 21, 1911, edition of the *Los Angeles Times* read. "By their inferior physical strength, they are unable to compete on an equal basis in any line of endeavor where ability is determined by sheer bodily prowess. All positions of physical power—such as in our police forces, our armies and our navies—will necessarily be filled by men. In other words, the enforcement of all law must inevitably rest with men. No law or ordinance could be effectually upheld except through the willingness of men to uphold it. And no matter what words were written on the statute books of any state, if the physical power (which is the masculine power) behind it were withdrawn, the law would immediately become void and impotent. Therefore, in equal suffrage we have the spectacle of women desiring to pass laws which they are physically incapable of upholding, and laws which they admit the men do not want."

A second editorial in the June 19, 1911, edition of the *Los Angeles Times* insisted that "Possession of the ballot will not help women, socially or industrially. It will make exactions upon her time and strength. It will invade the home and destroy its charm. It will not result in wiser laws or better government."

The loyal conductors of the California suffrage movement fought back against such limited thinking, meeting with politicians who believed giving women the vote would be disastrous. They hoped to persuade those opposed to the amendment to change their mind. Ellen Sargent encouraged the action and would have participated in the talks, too, if not for issues with her health. A letter from Susan Anthony written on June 2, 1905, encouraged Ellen to "not grow weary in the fight" and to "take heart knowing change is so close." Anthony shared memories of when she, Ellen, and Aaron met on the train in 1871 and asked her to recall how far the suffrage movement had come since that time. "How driven we were," Anthony wrote, "and look what has been accomplished."

Ellen Sargent passed away on July 13, 1911. She was eighty-five years old. On July 26, 1911, men and women united in a public gathering at Union Square in San Francisco to pay tribute to the suffrage leader. Among those at the celebration of her life was California congressman Thomas E. Hayden. Congressman Hayden told the people who came to pay their respects that "Mrs. Sargent was one of those wise elder women who saw years ago that women could not attain her highest development until she had the same large opportunities and the same large chance her brothers have."

The suffrage movement would miss Ellen Sargent's influence and work. Fellow advocates grieved the loss but pressed onward toward the goal of acquiring voting rights. The passage of the California suffrage amendment would be the ultimate way to honor Ellen's efforts for the cause. As the special elections approached, suffragists sought the opinion from various leading lights in politics on the probable results of the ballot. They received numerous messages of support.

United States senator John D. Works of Los Angeles told reporters at the *San Francisco Call* newspaper, "I predict a sweeping victory for the woman suffrage amendment, and, moreover, believe that its institution in this state will be nation wide in its effects." Dr. C. W. Chapman, mayor of Nevada City, California, noted, "I consider it but right and just that women should vote, and I want to be listed as an ardent supporter of the cause. It will certainly carry in this city." District Attorney Charles Tuttle of Placer County agreed and added that "the cause will win out in this country, and I am glad to be able to make the prediction. My belief is shared by Assemblyman Edward Gaylor, Ben Tabor of Auburn, Dr. Woodbridge of Roseville, Dr. Manson of Lincoln, and many others throughout the county who are in a position to know the weight and trend of local opinion."

On Friday, October 13, 1911, Amendment 8, the woman suffrage amendment, was narrowly passed. More than 121,500 voted for woman suffrage and 118,777 voted against. The effect the Golden State had on achieving women's rights played an important role in the passing of the Nineteenth Amendment to the United States Constitution in August 1920. The way suffrage leaders in California worked together with civic and social clubs to spread the word about women's fight for the vote was duplicated in the months to come and ultimately helped to gain the vote nationally. After the ballot was won in California, it was the objective of the suffrage leaders there to train other women in an understanding of political responsibility. Women in the Gold Country pressed forward to not only see that the Nineteenth Amendment was passed but also fought for improved property, marital, labor, and health rights. Women voters in California sought to live by the principle Susan B. Anthony shared on her many visits to the state. "Away with your man-visions," she told fellow suffragists. "Women propose to reject them all and begin to dream dreams for themselves."

CHAPTER SIX

Arizona and New Mexico: Two Paths to Suffrage

I think there will be no end to the good that will come by woman's suffrage, on the elected, on elections, on government, and on woman herself.

—CHIEF JUSTICE CHASE,
SIXTH CHIEF JUSTICE OF THE UNITED STATES

On September 18, 1909, Laura Gregg of the Arizona Equal Suffrage Campaign Committee rolled a sheet of letterhead into her typewriter and began an affectionate letter to Anna Howard Shaw, president of the National American Woman Suffrage Association. Shaw, who had been injured in an accident, was recuperating in Minneapolis, and Gregg wrote to her:

"If I had known that you were roasting on a bed of suffering in Minneapolis, I should certainly have sent you a little love note, as well as to send you all of the helpful thoughts that I could. At this late date, however, it is not too late to tell you how much I rejoice that your recovery has been so speedy, and that through it all you have had such Spartan courage to do such wonderful things as I am reading about, while you must have been suffering so much."

Shaw, as head of the biggest national organization promoting woman suffrage, had been traveling the country stumping for the cause and speaking from her heart to the state organizations that had sprung up in nearly every state and territory. She had won the hearts of her fellow suffragists with her warm and intelligent rhetoric and open attitudes. And while she was working on the national stage, organizations like the Arizona Equal Suffrage Campaign Committee were going into homes, posing legal arguments, asking questions, and changing minds.

In the late nineteenth and early twentieth centuries, as the territorial governments of the West formed and territorial laws were established, and then as territories made the move into statehood, suffrage advocates across the country had their eyes on the opportunities that came with crafting the law of the land from the ground up. If women hadn't been excluded from the vote by law in each territory, went the reasoning, they didn't need to be under the new laws and statutes that were being written.

After the Civil War, the discussion about women and the vote had been firmly on the political table for almost two decades. Women all over the United States had been protesting, lobbying, and had even been arrested for attempting to vote in elections. Pressure grew, as early as the 1870s, for a national suffrage amendment in Congress. But faced with great opposition—or apathy—on a nationwide scale, many suffrage advocates saw the laws being written on the frontier as the best chance for the vote to take hold in law.

Arizona Territory had been officially established in 1863, at the height of the Civil War. During the war years and Reconstruction, the battle over women's rights was first put on hold and was then brought to the national stage during the deliberations over the Fourteenth and Fifteenth Amendments to the Constitution. In the years leading up to the Civil War, women had been motivated by the work of Susan B. Anthony, Elizabeth Cady Stanton, and Lucretia Mott to think about what the vote would mean to women individually and to the issues faced by women and children in a changing world, such as labor laws, poverty, living conditions, and property rights.

The large swath of the American Southwest that had initially been New Mexico Territory, but was later separated into Arizona Territory and New Mexico Territory, was still sparsely populated in the 1880s and 1890s, though the influx of miners during the silver mining rush of the 1870s led to the development of boomtowns and attracted new residents. Cattle ranching was a growing industry in the territory, as well, and homesteads drew families as well as those looking to get rich quick.

The women of Arizona started forming their own suffrage organizations outside of the national structure during the territorial period. In 1891, Josephine Brawley Hughes joined with other women to create the first territorial organization devoted to the vote in preparation for Arizona's first bid for statehood. Perhaps taking a cue from its neighbor to the north, Utah Territory, the representatives to the constitutional convention heeded the demands of the women and included the vote as part of the state's proposed set of laws. When Arizona lost its bid for statehood, women lost as well.

Nearly every year thereafter when the legislature convened, another bill would be introduced, lobbied for by the women who supported suffrage, and would fail to succeed. In 1899, it seemed that the vote might be in their grasp when the lower house of the Arizona Territorial government passed a bill, but the upper house failed to do the same. Then, in the early 1900s, Frances Willard Munds became the chair of the Arizona Suffrage Association.

Arizona Territory was home to a number of Latter Day Saints, and Munds believed that joining forces with the Mormon women of the territory might make the difference to the cause. Munds was aware of the fact that the Utah Territory had made suffrage part of their constitution and had watched as Utah women lost and then regained suffrage when it achieved statehood. She knew that the Mormon Church had been

The National Association Opposed to Woman Suffrage

In the hundred years since woman suffrage became the universal law of the land, it has become easy to see the march across the West— and the battles in the East—as part of a predestined path toward the vote. But the reality was that woman suffragists faced opposition to their views at every turn—and even allies could sometimes prove problematic as priorities shifted and political strategies shifted to fit the argument of the day. Opposition to the vote was fierce and vocal. Tavern associations and brewers and distillers were against suffrage because of the close ties between votes for women and votes for Prohibition. Politicians feared shifting district demographics. Scientists—even some of the best—argued that women didn't have the mental capacity needed to make informed voting decisions. Husbands and fathers either felt that the votes of their wives and daughters would be redundant, or feared that they wouldn't. And over and over, the argument was made that women wouldn't "want" to vote. They wanted to keep to their sphere—the home and family, where their influence was felt every day. After all, "the hand that rocks the cradle rules the world."

Starting in about the 1860s, some of the opposition was organized around clubs and organizations—mostly at a local level. In places like Massachusetts, where the suffrage movement was gaining strength, the drive to actively agitate against woman suffrage was the strongest. One of the earliest groups to oppose the vote for women was the Massachusetts Association Opposed to the Further Extension of Suffrage to Women. However, no national organization existed that opposed the franchise—and most of the anti-suffrage actions were limited to mocking political cartoons and posters, harangues from the pulpit, and propaganda in the forms of articles and op-eds that professed the views of the anti-suffrage faction.

Even as the vote was sweeping across the West, there was no concerted, organized front fighting against it. There didn't need to

Fear mongering and ridicule were frequent parts of the fight to defeat woman suffrage. Library of Congress

be. The power of the vote was in the hands of male voters. Abigail Scott Duniway's individual lobby-and-persuade method seemed to be helping chip away at the opposition. Being in the right places at the right times was often helpful, too.

Washington, Idaho, California, Utah, Colorado, and Wyoming had all given women the vote after concerted efforts by suffragists and the political expediency in each of those states and territories by the time the National Association Opposed to Woman Suffrage (NAOWS) was founded by Josephine Dodge in 1911. Dodge was, interestingly, an early proponent of daycare for the children of working mothers. And her opposition to the vote—and the opposition of the organization—was based on her belief that giving women that political equality would decrease their civic involvement in social causes. Whether all who joined the movement agreed with that assessment, the national nature of the organization gave those against suffrage a focal point for their efforts. Like the national pro-suffrage groups, they organized local offices, printed pamphlets and posters, and held rallies and campaigns to promote their views.

The National Association Opposed to Woman Suffrage attracted male and some female supporters. Library of Congress

Ultimately, of course, the anti-suffragists failed—and the NAOWS, while it stayed active throughout the 1920s to oppose any progressive feminist agendas, faded into history.

influential in the decision. And she believed in the strength of women in numbers.

Munds's organization used many of the same tactics as those in other western states—combining public protest and media attention with personal lobbying. In 1903, a suffrage bill was finally passed by both houses of the legislature only to be vetoed by the governor. As Laura Gregg would report to Anna Howard Shaw in her 1909 letter, the women in favor of equality were not to be deterred. Gregg shared stories of going into homes, leading discussions, and even convincing anti-suffragists of the value of the vote for women.

When Arizona made its next bid for statehood, convening a constitutional convention in 1910, both the territorial advocates and the National Woman Suffrage Association made their strongest show of support yet

SIGNING THE DECLARATION OF THEIR INDEPENDENCE.

In the early nineteen-teens, as states began to jump on the suffrage bandwagon, the national press took notice. This 1911 illustration shows a group of women presenting their Declaration of Independence, which states "When in the course of female events it becomes necessary for women to have the ballot they're going to get it." Library of Congress

in an attempt to include the vote in the new constitution. Ultimately, the governor—Governor Alexander Brodie this time—objected to the inclusion out of concern that it would thwart the bid for statehood.

When Arizona's statehood was granted in February 1912, the constitution did not include the vote, but the momentum for its passage could not be stopped. Activists began their campaign to fix that almost immediately after statehood was finalized, introducing an initiative that was on the ballot that November. By the end of the year, Arizona women would have the right to vote, and eight years later the state would quickly ratify the Nineteenth Amendment, making the same true for women across the United States

To the east of Arizona, New Mexico was also going through growing pains in the early 1900s, facing many of the same challenges and struggles as they strove to achieve statehood. The suffrage movement in New Mexico had been slower to take hold, however, and the constitution adopted in 1910 in the run up to statehood posed obstacles to eventual suffrage that would be difficult to overcome.

Though the New Mexico constitution made it possible for the State Federation of Women's Clubs to lobby effectively for the vote in school elections and it provided full voting rights to men of Mexican and Hispanic descent, it was unusual in that it required a full three-fourths majority vote in every county to amend the constitution to grant woman suffrage. In New Mexico, the chances of suffrage passing by popular vote were slim. But on the national stage, Alice Paul and her militant Congressional Union were gathering supporters, and that network reached into the places in the West where the vote was still elusive.

New Mexico, which had long been part of Mexico and was still culturally more aligned with its southern neighbor in the mid-to-late eighteenth century, didn't embrace suffrage in the same way many of its western neighbors did. The Catholic Church, which had a heavy influence on the formerly Spanish territory, openly opposed woman

The national suffrage organizations and the states often worked closely together in the fight for amending the constitution. Here women are being dispatched to help the states with their campaigns for the vote: Rose Winslow and Lucy Burns to California, Doris Stevens and Ruth Astor Noyes to Colorado, Anna McGue to Washington, and Jane Pincus and Jessie H. Stubbs to Arizona. Library of Congress

suffrage in the nineteenth century, and the culture of male machismo in the region further stymied any attempts for the issue to get a toehold in discussions of women's rights in the new state's system of laws. What women's groups there were in the state didn't begin forming until the 1890s, and those tended to exclude Native and Hispanic women, who made up a significant percentage of the female population in the region.

Ella St. Clair Thompson, one of the strongest voices in the Congressional Union and the organization's Southern organizer, worked to garner support among the women's clubs in the state, and by 1915, a strong and growing network was in place in the region, helping to advocate for the national amendment. Thompson recognized the need to reach out to the Hispanic population of the region as well as to the Anglo ladies' clubs. She wrote to Alice Paul, "They say it is very difficult to get the

Spanish ladies out, but as I have one on the program to speak in Spanish, I think they will come—and their husbands as well." It was a smart and effective strategy in a place where there was strong political power held by Mexican American men. Soon flyers and speeches about the vote in New Mexico were bilingual, and women like Adelina Otero-Warren, who happened to be the niece of a the prominent head of the New Mexico Republican Party, lent their support to a strategy of personal lobbying of legislatures and public demonstrations on the national amendment, now known as the Susan B. Anthony Amendment. It was largely with the support of women like Otero-Warren that New Mexico would ratify the Nineteenth Amendment in 1920, but until then the women of the state were effectively silenced in state government. In 1920, however, they voted with enthusiasm—and Spanish-speaking women turned out in droves at the polls, making their voices heard loud and clear.

Alaska Territory and
Votes for Women

The second decade of the twentieth century saw the vote sweeping across the West as territories formed and then gained statehood in some cases, or as a result of decades of lobbying on the part of women's groups. Washington, 1910; California, 1911; Oregon, Arizona, and Kansas in 1912; and in 1913, the new territory of Alaska gave women the franchise.

Alaska had been part of the United States since its purchase from the Russian Empire in 1867, but it didn't become an organized territory with all of the political potential that implied until 1912. The huge region was home to Aleut and Inuit peoples and had seen Russian settlement and other small pockets of immigration from Asia and Europe since possibly the 1720s. After the Civil War, Secretary of State William Seward negotiated the purchase of the territory for $7.2 million, and thirty years later, when gold was discovered there, the investment paid off. Men flooded the region in search of riches, followed by women who saw opportunity in the new frontier.

When the territorial constitution was written in 1912, woman suffrage was not part of the document—but the examples from the Lower 48 held sway when, in 1913, Governor Walter Clark proposed woman suffrage for the territory and the men of the territory granted the franchise to all white women who were citizens, excluding indigenous people.

Alaska was on the forefront of voting rights for native peoples, too, and in 1915, the vote there was specifically extended to some indigenous peoples—though with the requirement that it only be extended to those who would give up their traditional ways for "civilization."

Since Alaska was a territory, it would not be part of the vote for national woman suffrage when it was ratified in 1920, but they had demonstrated the possibility of the state-by-state approach to achieving the vote by putting another "yes" on the map. And when Alaska was officially proclaimed a state on January 3, 1959, they had a long history of women's rights to bring with them to the union.

Alaska Territory, which had extended the franchise to women in 1913, was represeted by Margaret Vale, the niece of President Woodrow Wilson, in a suffrage parade in New York in October 1915. Library of Congress

CHAPTER SEVEN

—•◦•—

Nevada and Montana: A Black Mark on the Map

In the view of the terrible corruption of our politics, people ask, can we maintain universal suffrage? I say no, not without the aid of women.

—BISHOP GILBERT HAVEN,
BISHOP OF THE METHODIST EPISCOPAL CHURCH

By 1914, it seemed like a foregone conclusion that Montana women would soon have the right to vote, though in maps showing the progress of suffrage across the West it was featured, along with Nevada, as a large black mark. Though Montana's female population had enjoyed limited voting privileges, such as the right to vote in school elections, since territorial days, the right to vote in statewide elections and the right to hold office had remained elusive there and in Nevada, even as nine other western states and the Alaska Territory had written or changed their constitutions to include so-called "universal suffrage."

Women in Wyoming, the neighboring state to Montana's south, had been voting for forty-five years, when on November 3, 1914, Montana men—those who were white and over the age of twenty-one and thus eligible to vote—went to the polls to give the women of the state the same right. The Montanans may have been late to the party, but they were about to change history. Likewise in Nevada, men were finally ready to respond to the call for equality at the polls.

From 1895 through 1911, bills that would have put suffrage up for a general election vote were defeated or not even considered by the legislators in Helena. Then in 1913, perhaps bowing to the inevitable—or perhaps with the assumption that the male voters of the state would reject the proposition regardless—legislators agreed to put a constitutional amendment on the ballot in the next general election.

Montana's men had several weighty issues to decide in November 1914—an act establishing a state boxing commission, an initiative on workmen's compensation, the consolidation of the state universities, and the investment of permanent state funds. In many ways, it was a ballot that could have been put before the electorate in 2014, simple matters that had strong campaigns behind them. But the constitutional amendment had been decades in the making, and had required many thousands of hours of sweat and hard work. Women and their allies had been fighting for the vote for decades, and the 1914 victory involved hundreds of women from across the state, speaking out, talking to neighbors, mobilizing their chapters of the Woman's Christian Temperance Union, traveling the state, publishing leaflets, and fulfilling the promise made twenty-five years earlier when suffrage had been proposed by Perry McAdow during the 1889 constitutional convention. In the end, it was a close vote: 53 percent of voters—men—were in favor of equal suffrage. They had been convinced by their sisters, mothers, daughters, and neighbors.

A young Helena woman named Belle Fligelman had spread the word about suffrage while standing on soapboxes and preaching her message on street corners and in front of saloons in the capital city. Margaret Smith Hathaway became known as "the whirlwind," traveling the state from her home in Stevensville, Montana, via automobile and covering more than five thousand miles of Montana spreading the word about the vote. The women of the Missoula Teachers' Suffrage Committee would

Frieda Fligelman and Belle Fligelman Winestine

There is a statue of Jeannette Rankin in Montana's Capitol and in Washington D.C.'s Statuary Hall, but two young suffragists from Helena, Montana, stand as boldly in history as champions for the cause of women's rights. Frieda Fligelman, born in 1890, and her one-year-younger sister, Belle, were the only children in a prosperous, well-educated Jewish household, who grew up in the brand-new state of Montana. Both girls were sent to the University of Wisconsin for college degrees, and both championed the progressive causes popular in the first decades of the twentieth century.

Both young women worked for suffrage during their college years, and in 1914, Belle moved home to Helena, where she wrote articles on women's rights and other subjects for the Helena *Independent* and began stumping for both the vote and Jeannette Rankin's election to Congress in 1916. Belle literally stood on soap boxes on the capital city's street corners, scandalized her stepmother to the point that she threatened to evict Belle from the family home.

After Rankin's election, Belle moved to Washington, D.C., to serve as the congresswoman's secretary and speechwriter—four years before women would finally earn the franchise on a national scale. While in Washington, she became passionate about the need for women to fight for better conditions for women and children. She would never stop working toward her goals of equality, eventually running unsuccessfully for Montana's state senate in 1932.

Frieda Fligelman enrolled at Columbia University to study sociology after graduating from the University of Wisconsin. After World War II, she returned to Helena and founded the Institute for Social Logic—a think tank intended to examine the way public policies are formed. Belle, who had married Norman Winestine, had also returned to Helena to raise children and work on women's rights and child welfare. The sisters would be lifelong advocates for women's rights and were active in the American Association of University Women, the League of Women Voters, and other public organizations that supported equality under the law. In the run-up to the 1914 election, Belle worked with Lora Edmunds and Mary O'Neill to publish the *Suffrage Daily News*, a four-page daily that argued for the vote that included contributions from men and women and coverage of big events like the Suffrage Parade led by Jeannette Rankin in September 1914 down the main street of Helena.

print and distribute thirty thousand flyers. And many other women stepped up to lobby their friends, spouses, fathers, and sons.

Other factors were at play in Montana, as well, including the state's early twentieth century bent toward progressive national politics during the campaign for "the vote." A number of reformers were interested in curbing the interests of the powerful industrialists, like the Anaconda Company, which had consolidated its operations in Butte and was known to be buying votes in the legislature, as well as the newspapers that reported on as the company and the mines that provided its ore. Some progressives believed that women voters would help check the influence of the company.

Another important influence on the suffrage vote might have been the wave of homesteaders who came to the state after 1909 when a significant number of women homesteaders were drawn by the promise of free land under the expansion of the Homestead Act, including a significant number of woman homesteaders, including single women. Homesteaders generally seemed to be pro-suffrage—perhaps representing the egalitarian atmosphere of the West. In a state where women worked right alongside men in similar professions, it was difficult to argue against giving them the same rights.

In 1916, Montana's most famous woman suffragist, Jeannette Rankin, would be elected to the U.S. House of Representatives. A progressive Republican from Missoula, Rankin would become famed for her votes against U.S. entry into both world wars from the floor of the U.S. House of Representatives. Rankin was a member of a prominent Missoula, Montana, family—privileged, educated, wealthy, tenacious, and compassionate. She felt personally drawn to the world of social work and, through that, to progressive politics. Her hands-on experience with social work frustrated her in its seeming futility. She felt that rather than face the dirt and poverty of women and children on a case-by-case basis, a better route to helping the poor would be through not just securing the vote

Jeannette Rankin, the first woman elected to the U.S. House of Representatives, appears on the balcony at the National American Woman Suffrage Association. Library of Congress

for women but through holding political office herself. Rankin reasoned that more women in office would mean more women working for equal pay, better working conditions, and education and sanitation. She went to work on suffrage campaigns in Washington State, and was instrumental in helping women there gain the right to vote in 1910. Back in Montana, she mobilized the women of the state as the state secretary for the National Woman Suffrage Association. She lobbied the legislature, she organized letter-writing campaigns, and she reached across the aisle when Democratic, mostly pro-vote candidates won a majority in the 1912 election. Just before the legislature opened in early 1913, she organized a statewide suffrage meeting in the capital city, keeping the issue front and center. When the election of 1914 was behind her and women had the right to vote, Rankin turned her attention to holding statewide office herself.

In Nevada, the campaign for women's right to vote had begun shortly after statehood in 1864, but fifty years later, the Nevada Equal Franchise

Society was working to get voters to come to the polls to support their cause. Much as was the case in the state of Montana, Nevada had relatively few voters scattered over a vast area of land. Determined to visit miners, sheepherders and cattle ranchers, tavern owners, farmers, and townsfolk everywhere to give a personal message about woman suffrage, women traveled widely handing out flyers and shaking hands. Newspaper stories about their efforts were part of the campaign as well.

Much like other western states, the issue of suffrage in Nevada had been debated many times since the drafting of the state constitution, which specifically prohibited women from the vote in 1864. In 1869, however, as Wyoming Territory was granting the right to its female citizens, Curtis Hillyer proposed an amendment to the Nevada constitution in favor of suffrage. The measure passed both houses and spurred the conversation among Nevada's citizens but was not ratified. The first Nevada suffrage convention happened at Battle Mountain in 1870, and one year later, the legislature again failed to ratify the 1869 amendment. Over the next two decades, the issue was raised again and again and narrowly defeated. And then, in 1890, Susan Miller, Josephine Taylor, and six more women were elected to school positions. In 1893, an act was passed allowing women to serve as attorneys, and in 1895, after Reverend Mila Tupper Maynard spoke at the Nevada Assembly in support of the vote, the legislature passed a resolution that was once again not ratified.

Even through these fits and starts, the women of Nevada were making great strides in the quest for equality. Women started suffrage organizations, voted in school elections in limited cases, and were elected to hold school trusteeships. Then in 1899, the legislature not only failed to pass a suffrage bill, they also outlawed the right of women to run for county school superintendent, a right they had enjoyed for decades.

Over the next ten years, Nevada women watched as five legislatures convened and adjourned without making a move toward equal suffrage, and legislation and the men of the state continued to regulate what roles they could serve in public education. Finally, in 1909, the tide seemed to turn in their favor. Nevada women were legally allowed to serve as school superintendents and notaries, and in 1911, Margaret Stanislawsky stepped up to serve as the first president of the Nevada Equal Franchise Society, leading to the introduction of legislation during the 1911 session.

The grassroots movement and use of the press was underway. As had been effective in other western states, Nevada used a multipronged approach to encourage men to vote for suffrage. County-based chapters

The mainstream press and specialist publications like The Suffragist *helped spread the word about equal suffrage. Women worked tirelessly to put positive messages in the hands of the male voters who would determine their fate.* Library of Congress

Mila Tupper Maynard: Nevada Minister and Suffragist

As a little girl, Mila Tupper dreamed of being a Unitarian minister in an era where most women were still encouraged to keep silent in church. Born in 1864 in Iowa, she would go on to study theology at Cornell and was ordained as a Unitarian pastor the year of her graduation, in 1889. She then returned to the Midwest to serve churches in Indiana and Michigan, where she met her husband, Rezin Maynard. Maynard had been a trustee of the Grand Rapids church where Mila had been serving, and in 1893, after moving to Reno, Nevada, the two became co-pastors of a Unitarian Church in the fledgling city.

Mila had proved herself to be willing to stand against societal norms by becoming a minister in the first place. Rezin Maynard proved a worthy companion in her fight for social justice, supporting Mila when she lectured and taught courses at the University of Nevada and speaking out with her on social justice issues such as women's rights—and woman suffrage specifically.

In 1895, Mila addressed the Nevada State Assembly to support the legislature's "temporary" suffrage measure To support her, Rezin wrote an opinion piece, published in the *Reno Evening Gazette*, which declared that allowing women the vote would cause a "complete revolution in government, religion, and social life."

The Maynards would eventually move to Utah, where Mila would continue to enjoy the franchise, and then moved on to Los Angeles. Both continued to teach and to minister throughout their lives. When Mila died in 1926, it was with the knowledge that her dreams of reform, though perhaps they had started on a very personal level with her dreams of the ministry, had come true for all American women.

of the Nevada Equal Franchise Society were started all over the state, and in 1912, the society put pressure on candidates for the legislature, urging them to support the suffrage resolution. On Election Day of that year, they stood by polls and reminded voters to support those candidates who had pledged to do so.

Nevada's slow and deliberate process of approving legislation finally paid off in 1913, when the resolution passed in 1911 was approved. In 1914 the question of woman suffrage would finally go before the voters in a year where the people of Nevada mobilized on both sides of the issue. The Men's Business League had long been antagonistic to the question of the franchise, but the Nevada Men's Suffrage League was formed to counteract its effects, and when a man named George Wingfield spoke out against suffrage, newspapers across the state mocked his

Congressional Union's summer headquarters—note the map of success in the background —1914. Library of Congress

backward attitudes. More pro-suffrage societies were founded and advocates were out en masse.

Nevada's caution meant that it would be two more years before women could vote in statewide elections—but in 1915, they voted in city elections and formed civic organizations that fulfilled the promise they'd made when arguing for the vote. In 1916, Nevada's women stepped up to the ballot box in county and state elections and made their way onto the ballots. The black marks on the map of suffrage in the West were gone.

Chapter Eight

———•◦•———

The March across the Great Plains

I think women are bound to seek the suffrage as a very great means of doing good.
    —Frances Power Cobbe, Irish Writer, Social Reformer, and Leading Women's Suffrage Campaigner

From 1912 to 1920, the voting map shifted with astonishing rapidity after the long years of the late nineteenth century when progress had seemingly stalled. The political exigencies of the Civil War and Reconstruction had made way for the reforming zeal of progressives at the turn of the twentieth century, and while war in Europe was on the horizon, the Gilded Age and industrialization had swept across the nation, allowing citizens a chance to participate in clubs and political organizations at a new level. And the expansion of states into the West had opened new opportunities for the people to have a voice in shaping laws. By 1912, decades had passed since the voters of Wyoming Territory had allowed women not only to step to the ballot box but also to appear on those ballots. Women all over the country had joined civic organizations in record numbers—the Woman's Christian Temperance Union (WCTU), pro-suffrage organizations, as well as anti-suffrage organizations. The direst of predictions about what having masculine responsibilities would do to

Carrie Nation

The barroom at the Hotel Carey in Wichita, Kansas, was extremely busy most nights. Cowhands and trail riders arrived by following the smell of whiskey and the sound of an inexperienced musician playing an out-of-tune piano inside the saloon. Beyond the swinging doors awaited a host of well-used female companions and an assortment of alcohol to help drown away the stresses of life on the rugged plains. Patrons were too busy drinking, playing cards, and flirting with soiled doves to notice the stout, six-foot-tall woman enter the saloon. She wore a long, black alpaca dress and bonnet and carried a Bible. Almost as if she were offended by the obvious snub, the matronly newcomer loudly announced her presence. As it was December 23, 1900, she shouted, "Glory to God! Peace on earth and good will to men!"

At the end of her proclamation, she hurled a massive brick at the expensive mirror hanging behind the bar and shattered the center of it. As the stunned bartender and customers looked on, she pulled an iron rod from under her full skirt and began tearing the place apart.

The sheriff was quickly summoned, and soon the violent woman was being escorted out of the bar and marched to the local jail. As the door on her cell was slammed shut and locked, she shouted out to the men, "You put me in here a cub, but I will go out a roaring lion and make all hell howl."

Carrie Nation's tirade echoed throughout the Wild West. For decades the lives of women from Kansas to California had been adversely affected by the abuse of alcohol by their husbands, fathers, and brothers. Nation was one of the first to take such a public, albeit violent, stance against the problem. The Bible-thumping, brick-and-bat-wielding Nation was a member of the WCTU. The radical organization, founded in 1874, encouraged wives and mothers distressed over the effects of alcohol to join in the crusade against liquor and the sellers of the vile drink.

Carrie Nation. Library of Congress

In 1877, Nation became a member of the WCTA, which protested drinking and fought for the enforcement of state liquor laws which forbade the sale or manufacture of alcohol. The WCTU was concerned about the destructive power of alcohol and the problems it was causing families and societies.

The methods employed by the WCTU were generally nonviolent. They would gather outside bars and sing hymns. The tactic was often successful, and many bars closed as a result. Carrie Nation had a terrific grudge against alcohol and those who sold it and could not be persuaded to protest in a civil manner. She had married two men who would not give up the bottle.

Nation had been born Carrie Amelia Moore on November 26, 1846, in Garrard County, Kentucky. Her father was an itinerant minister who moved his wife and children from Kentucky to Texas, then on to Missouri and back again to Kentucky.

Although women were disenfranchised at the time, WCTU's organization and infrastructure were essential to early Prohibition Party success. The WCTU and Carrie Nation proved the power women had and helped support the idea that those women should have the right to vote.

women had not come to fruition. Instead there had been a great awakening about the potential and abilities of the half of the population that had been silenced for so long.

In the West, where women found greater acceptance in the professions and demonstrated their grit amid the hardships of the frontier, the vote had happened quickly in the grand scheme of things. Perhaps the looser constraints of a less regimented social structure had contributed to women participating in all sorts of activities outside of their traditionally proscribed sphere, including political campaigns. Women worked for the candidates of their choice, for social reforms including the prohibition of alcohol, and for the vote. Their campaigns covered scattered voters stretched over millions of square miles—but the personal approach advocated by suffragists in some of the western states had proved to be effective. Women were lobbying their neighbors and their legislators personally to make the case for equality. And the public arm of the suffrage movement had gained hard-earned acceptance in many places.

The fashionable women of Lawrence, Kansas, lobby for votes. Library of Congress

Across the Great Plains, particularly in the middle West, the WCTU had reached its long fingers into the more organized churches, schools, and town structures crying for the reform that the vote could bring. Kansas passed a suffrage amendment in 1912, even before its wilder neighbors to the west, propelled by the reform zeal of women like Carrie Nation. Illinois followed in 1913. South Dakota had been debating and rejecting suffrage since its territorial days, but it would grant the vote to women in 1918, a year after its sibling North Dakota offered presidential suffrage to the women of that state. Nebraska also took the presidential route, giving women the right to vote for the man who would hold that office in 1917. Many other states opted for that introduction to the franchise for women, offering the chance to vote in presidential elections before the national amendment would grant the unlimited right in 1920. Illinois, Missouri, Minnesota, Wisconsin, Iowa, and other states east of the Mississippi were all beginning to push the door open in that way by 1919.

Part of the reason for the shift was that even before the Great War, women in the cities began entering the workforce in growing numbers, taking on jobs in numerous professional fields as well as continuing to work in the more traditionally feminine occupations. As a result, women's economic status had undergone a significant transformation, and as skirt hems lifted, the arguments against the vote seemed to fall away. Politics—and the anti-progressive attitudes toward Prohibition and labor laws and social welfare programs—still stood in the way of equality, but the arguments against the vote became thinner and thinner.

After Kansas had been famously admitted to the Union as a free state in November 1861, the pain and strife of the Civil War held its grip over state politics, as it did the rest of the country. Largely due to the efforts of Clarina Nichols, a New Englander who had emigrated to Kansas in the 1850s and who introduced the idea of universal suffrage at the state's constitutional convention in 1859 and other leaders in the suffrage movement, women had the right to vote in Kansas school elections

On May 6, 1911, Inez Milholland and two other women lifted a banner before a crowd of three thousand marchers up Fifth Avenue in New York City, proclaiming, "Forward out of error, Leave behind the night; Forward through the darkness, Forward into light." When they reached Union Square, speakers from the parade's marchers addressed a crowd of ten thousand. With the vote sweeping across the West, some suffragists and anti-suffragists alike were beginning to feel that a national suffrage amendment was inevitable. But the battle was far from over.

Woman suffrage was, indeed, gaining support all over the country. Women had been voting in presidential primaries and local elections based on territorial and state law for decades, but it had yet to move beyond the campaign phase in most places in the East. In New York City, the number of people who had turned out to march had tripled over the previous year. And the national conversation was shifting, partly due to the roll of the vote across the West and partly due to new groups that were about to be involved in the story.

In 1912, when Theodore Roosevelt was running for reelection on the Bull Moose Party ticket, his was one of the first major voices in the national political establishment in favor of a Suffrage Amendment. Perhaps buoyed by that, the New York City suffrage parade drew twenty thousand supporters that year.

The next year, 1913, saw a major suffrage parade down Pennsylvania Avenue in Washington, D.C. Organized by the National American Woman Suffrage Association (NAWSA), it offered a major spectacle for supporters of suffrage to rally around, and the fight was about to heat up. A young suffragist named Alice Paul, a Quaker who had worked in England for suffrage, stepped up. She would form the Congressional Union, later named the National Woman's Party (NWP), in opposition to what she felt were the ineffective tactics and slow pace of the NAWSA. Adopting more militant tactics like picketing, hunger strikes, and massive rallies intended to draw support, Paul's group was inspired by the more confrontational style of the English suffragists. Her efforts reinvigorated the movement among younger women. And Paul became famous for her attacks on President Woodrow Wilson's failure to support suffrage.

As Europe became embroiled in war and the political conversation in the United States shifted to the issue of neutrality or intervention, the NWP and NAWSA didn't relent in their push for the vote. Perhaps they had learned from the delays of the Civil War and the rift in its wake, because in 1915, Carrie Chapman Catt, a former president of the NAWSA who had been active in the movement since the 1880s, took over the organization's leadership again. Catt's "Winning Plan" strategy focused on a state-by-state approach, similar to what had been happening in the West.

Though the campaigns were rarely coordinated, and often seemed to be in opposition to each other, Catt's state-by-state approach and Paul's political protests at the same time that Woodrow Wilson decided to enter World War I provided the final push. Woman suffragists argued that not only was it time for the vote, the lack of it might keep women from full participation in the war effort. Wilson reluctantly endorsed suffrage and in 1918, the House of Representatives, urged by Representative Jeannette Rankin from the state of Montana, passed a suffrage amendment. In 1919, the Senate followed suit, and ratification began.

Tennessee became the thirty-sixth and deciding state to approve the Nineteenth Amendment on August 18, 1920.

Women on the plains had long proved their mettle as pionneers, working alongside their husbands and fathers on homesteads. By the early twentieth century, they would be moving into the workforce in greater numbers. Library of Congress

starting in the year of statehood. But in 1867, during the painful period of Reconstruction, the first postwar attempt to extend the franchise statewide emerged when Governor Crawford and the State Impartial Suffrage Association introduced an amendment to the state constitution that would grant the vote to women and blacks.

When the vote on the amendment failed and the Fourteenth and Fifteenth Amendments were ratified without extending the franchise to women, Kansas women adopted the strategy of building on their school-voting rights by working toward gaining the vote in municipal elections. Over the next twenty years, the Kansas Equal Suffrage Association pushed for the rights of women to use the ballot and appear on it. In 1887, Kansas women not only earned the right to vote in citywide elections, they took seats on city councils. In Syracuse, Kansas, five women were elected to the city council. And In Argonia, Susanna Madora Salter became the first woman mayor in the United States.

Much as in other states during the Gilded Age of the late nineteenth and early twentieth centuries, the early victories of Kansas's women voters were stalled when it came to the wider franchise. But as campaigns gained momentum across the West and the national fight became part of the national media frenzy, Kansas voters had the opportunity to vote again on a suffrage amendment, finally ratifying it in November 1912. The suffrage movement of Kansas, the eighth state to grant full suffrage to women, didn't stop at the state borders. Kansas woman suffrage advocates, including the governor and other leading lights on the issue, lent their aid to the national suffrage movement and voted to ratify it fewer than two weeks after the Nineteenth Amendment was finally proposed by Congress.

CHAPTER NINE

---◦●◦---

War Work and National Suffrage

*When you were weak and I was strong, I toiled for you. Now you
are strong and I am weak. Because of my work for you, I ask your
aid, I ask the ballot for myself and my sex. As I stood by you, I
pray you stand by me and mine.*

—CLARA BARTON, PIONEERING NURSE WHO FOUNDED THE
AMERICAN RED CROSS, TO THE SOLDIERS.

Among the busy men sitting at rows of welding machines at the
Standifer-Clarkson Shipyard in Vancouver, Washington, in 1917,
were several equally busy women. All were dressed in drab gray or
brown clothing, work boots, heavy canvas aprons, and off-white, tri-
angular scarves covered their heads. Sparks flew from the metal pieces
being fused together to be used to build ships that would be dispatched
to fight in the war in Europe. The assassination of Archduke Franz Ferdinand of Austria-Hungary in June 1914 propelled the major European
military powers toward war. Gavrilo Princip, a Yugoslav nationalist,
was responsible for Ferdinand's death. His actions prompted Austria-
Hungary to declare war on Serbia. European nations aligned themselves
with the side of the argument they favored, and fighting ensued for more
than three years before the United States entered the conflict. Germany's

atrocities during this time forced the United States to declare war on the country in April 1917. Hundreds of thousands of American men were enlisted to fight, leaving numerous vacancies in the workforce. Women were recruited to fill those positions. Some of those positions were in shipyards such as the Standifer-Clarkson Shipyard.

Despite the prevailing idea among traditionalists that women should stay out of the workforce, World War I made the need for labor so urgent that women were hired in record numbers. In addition to taking jobs in department stores, railroads, and with the postal department, women answered the call to be employed as police officers, firefighters, munitions workers. By the spring of 1918, munitions factories were the largest employer of American women.

When it came to serving their country, women proved they were equal to men. The employment of women supported the war. Women worked not only as nurses but also as ambulance drivers, in steel mills, and in the textile industry. Women across the nation were doing their part to help. Although some political leaders recognized their contributions and were grateful, they still were not convinced granting women the vote was right for the country.

By the time the United States had entered World War I, all the western states had achieved women's suffrage at some level, but securing the right for women to vote in every state continued to be a struggle. The comments about that struggle by Lucy Burns, a leader of the NWP, were echoed by women everywhere. "It's unthinkable that a national government which represents women should ignore the issue of the right of all women to be politically free," Burns noted. Regardless of the battle being fought abroad, key suffragist leaders such as Harriot Stanton Blatch (daughter Elizabeth Cady Stanton), Alice Paul, and Lucy Burns believed women needed to continue to fight for their rights on the home front.

Women in the western portion of the United States were dedicated to securing the vote for women throughout the country, and they were

"Would the Soldier Give Her the Ballot? was an illustration created by Oscar Cesare for the New York Post *in 1917 when the suffrage movement and the war were very much a part of the national consciousness.* Library of Congress

Lucy Burns. Library of Congress

also working to change the prewar prejudices that defined the boundaries between "men's work" and "women's work." Women working in shipyards and in munitions plants proved they could do the job, and it forced authors of training manuals, dispersed at various factories, to revise the wording of the material. For example, the instructions for operating an engine lathe had to be changed to show what women had done with the tool.

"The operations of rough turning and finishing the profile together with the boring of the cavity have now been carried out by women in all parts of the country and with complete success.

"In the roughing operations, the women have proved to be capable of operating not only one lathe, but two.

"It is not suggested that women be asked to operate two machines as a rule. The sole object of this and the foregoing example is to show that, if one woman can continuously operate two machines, the handling of one machine is, without doubt, a perfectly simple achievement."

Although the manuals were being updated by men to include women's influence on the line, the attitude about their female presence in the factories was far from accepting. The hope of the leaders of the suffrage movement was that the momentum the cause had gained since America entered World War I would continue to grow and eventually lead the country to embrace a new perspective about women.

There were several women in key positions with suffrage groups that were helping to influence the public in 1917. Carrie Chapman Catt, head of the National American Woman Suffrage Association, was one of the brightest stars in the movement. She continually made the front page of newspapers such as the *Los Angeles Times* and the *Salt Lake Tribune*, urging the passing of the suffrage amendment. Born in Ripon, Wisconsin, in 1859, Catt became interested in women's rights when she learned at the age of seven that women were not allowed to vote. She excelled in school, and despite her father's initial objection to Carrie attending college, she enrolled at Iowa State Agriculture College in Ames, Iowa. She graduated with a degree in General Science for Women. Catt moved to California to become the first female journalist for a San Francisco newspaper. She quit her job as a reporter when her boss began to harass her. After that experience, Catt vowed to improve women's lives. She became a public speaker advocating for reform with regards to women's rights. In 1889, members of the Iowa Woman Suffrage Association sought Catt out and asked her to become the state organizer and recording secretary.

Catt became a powerful speaker for the suffrage movement and was a much-needed younger voice. The founders of the woman's movement, Susan B. Anthony, Elizabeth Cady Stanton, and Lucy Stone, were in their

Carrie Chapman Catt. Library of Congress

mid-seventies. They had been fighting for decades and saw the importance of new faces and new ideas within the movement. Catt was one
of the younger women tasked with taking their place in the continuing
struggle to gain the vote. Susan B. Anthony recruited Catt to the national
platform in 1892, and that same year Carrie began traveling to different
cities in the United States, giving speeches on why women should be
allowed at the polls. Catt worked for woman's suffrage for more than
twenty-five years before America joined World War I. Touring Europe
to study woman's suffrage there, she rose in the ranks of the NAWSA,
alongside other forceful suffragists such as Molly Hay and Alice Paul.

Catt's comments about the United States going to war were covered
extensively in West Coast newspapers. At a suffrage rally in Ohio on May
14, 1917, Catt criticized political leaders for presenting the country as "a
champion of democracy when it is only a democracy for half its people."
She noted that it was "unthinkable that mothers who would be giving
their sons to fight the battle of humanity were not entitled to be a part
in the deliberations of the government." She contended that the United
States had no right to talk about "making the world safe for democracy
as long as it believed in drawing the sex line.

"We had better blot the mote from our own eye before we go forth
and try to blot it from the Prussian eye," she added. "There is nothing
more illogical than to insist that men have the divine right to rule over
the women and say at the same time kings haven't divine right to rule
over man."

While Carrie Chapman Catt and delegates of the NAWSA representing all the western states were marching, petitioning, and delivering
speeches about how women were worthy of the vote, more and more
women were entering the workforce. Every man who marched off to
war left behind a job needing to be filled. Not only were women taking
over those jobs in their communities, but some were also joining various branches of the military. More than eleven thousand females joined

the navy between 1917 and 1919. Many more women served as army and navy nurses, and thousands offered their time and talents to the American Red Cross and the Salvation Army. The duties women were assuming further fueled the argument that women had secured a place in society and deserved to vote. Suffrage marches held from San Francisco, California, to San Antonio, Texas, called attention to the absence of women at the polls and the need for reform. Banners with slogans that read "Woman Suffrage Going Not Coming" were displayed in cities and towns across the country. Some applauded the idea and others dismissed the notion out right.

"You frequently hear uninformed people say: 'Woman suffrage is coming sooner or later—you might as well make up your mind to it,'" read one newspaper column opposed to giving women the right to vote. "Nothing could be further from the truth," the May 25, 1916, edition of the *Daily Times* read. "The elections held in the last four or five years indicate that the mass of the people are awake to the folly of forcing the vote on women. Here is the Record: Ohio defeated Woman Suffrage in 1912 by 87,455; Ohio defeated Woman Suffrage in 1914 by 182,905; Michigan defeated Woman Suffrage in 1912 by 760; Michigan defeated Woman Suffrage in 1913 by 96,144; Wisconsin defeated Woman Suffrage in 1912 by 91,478; North Dakota defeated Woman Suffrage in 1914 by 9,139; Nebraska defeated Woman Suffrage in 1914 by 10,104; Missouri defeated Woman Suffrage in 1914 by 140,206; Pennsylvania defeated Woman Suffrage in 1915 by 55,686; New Jersey defeated Woman Suffrage in 1915 by 51,108; Massachusetts defeated Woman Suffrage in 1915 by 133,447; New York defeated Woman Suffrage in 1915 by 194,984."

Suffragists like Abbie E. Krebs of California and Sara Bard Field of Oregon helped to rally women together in the western states to bring about change in locations where females had fought for suffrage to be placed on the ballot and political leaders voted against it. All held to the

Promotional poster meant to gain women's aid in World War I. Library of Congress

belief that unless woman's suffrage was passed in all states, women were still being denied their liberty.

On June 7, 1916, suffragists across the nation met in Chicago to attend a meeting of the Committee on Resolutions of the Republican National Convention. Several delegates took to the dais to be heard on the subject of equal suffrage. Among those present was Carrie Chapman Catt. Carrie proposed that the "Republican party reaffirm its faith in government of the people, for the people by favoring the extensions of suffrage to women as a measure of justice to one half of the adult population of the country." The suffragists in the coliseum where the convention was taking place erupted with applause. Harriot Stanton Blatch of Kansas, a member of the Congressional Union for Woman Suffrage, took the platform next and gave a speech that prompted the same response Catt's had received. "The biggest and most admirable thing the Republican Party had done has been to write the Fourteenth and Fifteenth Amendments into the Constitution," Blatch reminded the committee. "You have stood by the black man, now we want you to stand by the women."

Support for woman's suffrage was on the rise just prior to the United States entering the war. Support gained by liquor lobbyists was greater, however, and encouraged constituents to vote against suffrage. Suffrage leaders in the West appealed to their representatives in those states to intercede on behalf of the movement and convince Washington that the issue of woman's right to vote should be a national issue and not simply up to the states as was so many times given as the reason for not acting.

The executive board of the NAWSA decided they needed to take its case to the men running for president of the United States in the 1916 election. Just before the annual convention held in September 1916, invitations were issued to the Democratic incumbent, President Woodrow Wilson, and the Republican candidate, Charles E. Hughes. Hughes declined the invitation, but Woodrow Wilson agreed to be at the event.

According to the September 9, 1916, edition of the *Pittsburgh Daily Post*, President Wilson arrived at the convention shortly before six o'clock on September 8 to deliver his address to the NAWSA. An orchestra played "The Star-Spangled Banner" as he approached the podium, and all the women delegates from coast to coast stood up and cheered. The theater was packed with women, but there were a few men present. "The astonishing thing about this movement," President Woodrow Wilson told an enthusiastic crowd, "is not that it has grown so slowly, but that it has grown so rapidly. Two decades ago, no doubt Madam President will agree with me in saying, it was a handful of women who were fighting this cause. Now it is a great multitude of women who are fighting it.

"I get a little impatient sometimes about the discussion of the channels and methods by which change must prevail. And I assure you, it will prevail. . . . It is not merely because women are discontented. It is because women have seen visions of duty, land that is something that we not only cannot resist, but, if we are true Americans, we do not wish to resist. . . . I have not come to fight for you, but with you, and in the end I think we shall not quarrel over the method."

The crowd was overjoyed with hope and applauded and cheered the president. For Carrie Chapman Catt and all the delegates, it seemed at long last they had an ally of great importance and that gaining the vote was within reach.

On April 2, 1917, suffragists learned they would have to wait a little longer before the issue would be heard in the joint houses of Congress. The United States was now a part of World War I. President Wilson asked Carrie Chapman Catt to be part of the Woman's Committee of the Council of National Defense. Washington state delegate Susie Smith was made the chair of the group, which addressed issues of child welfare, education, food production, and many others. Carrie accepted the job but continued to press for woman's suffrage to be addressed.

Women of all ages worked to support woman suffrage in the early 1900s. This photo, taken circa 1917, purports to feature the "Oldest Suffragette." By 1917, the Susan B. Anthony Amendment had been nearly fifty years in the making. Library of Congress

Congress refused to discuss any bills or issues except war efforts during its spring 1917 session. Suffragists were furious with the government and President Wilson's administration for once again putting the crucial matter on the back burner. Carrie Chapman Catt summoned women from across the country to join her in New York to march and collect signatures in favor of the suffrage amendment. Other supporters of woman's right to vote decided to picket the White House. Alice Paul and her followers paraded back and forth in front of the president's office, carrying signs that read: "Mr. President, How Long Must Women Wait for Liberty?" and "Mr. President, What Will You Do for Woman Suffrage?" Alice Paul and the thousand-plus women with her picketed for more than a year. In addition to enduring taunts and jeers from spectators opposed to suffrage, the women were arrested and kept in jail for several months. While behind bars, Paul organized a hunger strike to protest the harsh treatment of innocent people.

Protests like the one Alice Paul initiated were among the most recognizable events in the suffrage movement. Lesser known state suffrage associations in the western states worked tirelessly to keep the suffrage issue at the forefront of the public and political leaders' minds. All those efforts combined helped to persuade President Wilson to put his full weight behind the fight for woman's enfranchisement. "We have made partners of women in this war," President Wilson told members of the House of Representatives. "Shall we admit them only to partnership of suffering and sacrifice and toil and not to a partnership of privilege, and right?"

In early January 1918, an amendment extending the vote to women was introduced to lawmakers by Montana congresswoman Jeannette Rankin. The House gallery was crowded with concerned citizens in support of the bill. Carrie Chapman Catt was there along with many other suffragists. All were anxious to hear the issue debated. On January 9, 1918, President Wilson once again emphasized to the Senate his

Suffragist in her jail cell. Library of Congress

support for the suffrage amendment, stating it was "an act of right and justice" as well as a "vitally necessary war measure."

Congresswoman Rankin opened the session, and the women packed into the galleries cheered enthusiastically when she stood up to address her colleagues. "How shall we answer this challenge, gentlemen?" she began. "How can we explain to the world if the Congress that voted to make the world safe for democracy refuses to give this small measure of democracy to the women of this country?" Her comments were received with resounding applause. "Today as never before, the nation needs these women—needs the work of every woman and their hearts, hands, and minds. All the energy must be utilized in the most effective service they can give. Are we now going to refuse these women the opportunity to serve in the face of their pleas? In the face of the nation's greatest need?"

Detail from photo of the 65th Congress of the United States, March 1918. Jeannette Rankin stands alone as the only woman in the house. Library of Congress

Once President Wilson reiterated that he was fully behind the Susan B. Anthony Suffrage Amendment, it was decided the bill would be voted on that afternoon. Jubilant suffrage leaders across the nation declared that the president's open advocacy of their cause made victory sure. When he urged a delegation of anti-suffrage democratic representatives to vote for the amendment, it was the first decisive public stand in favor of congressional action on suffrage. The amendment passed the House with just one vote more than the two-thirds required.

While waiting for the amendment to be presented and debated in the Senate, women in California suffrage organizations continued their work in helping to secure the vote for women in the East. A Bureau of Information and Correspondence was established in Los Angeles under the direction of Mrs. Seward A. Simons, the California congressional chairwoman for the National Suffrage Association. The bureau would provide any individual or state politician east of the Mississippi with data on suffrage and the way it worked in California and other states where suffrage had been granted. They hoped the information would convince leaders in states where women weren't able to vote to change their minds about suffrage.

The National Woman's Party of Utah met in Salt Lake to discuss the ratification of the suffrage amendment and the far-reaching implications the passing of the bill would have on women throughout the state and women's war work in the field. Suffragists in Oregon met to compile a series of questions for those individuals running for office in the state. All candidates for office who if elected might have a voice in furthering the cause of equal suffrage needed to be scrutinized thoroughly. Going forward, it would be essential to ask all candidates for the United States Senate and Congress their attitudes toward the Susan B. Anthony Suffrage Amendment. Only those who committed to supporting the cause would have their support.

Women from Astoria, Oregon, to Austin, Texas, took the message of suffrage to neighborhoods, parks, and public thoroughfares to spread the word that females should at long last be allowed to vote. Dedicated suffragists urged citizens to contact their senators and encourage them to vote in favor of the Susan B. Anthony Amendment. The Senate would hold debates and discuss the bill in late September 1918. As of August, the amendment was two votes short of the two-thirds necessary to pass.

On October 1, 1918, President Wilson addressed the Senate in favor of suffrage. He told elected officials that he "regarded the extension of suffrage to women as vitally essential to the successful prosecution of the great war of humanity in which the country was engaged." Despite the long, hard work of women across the nation and the president's support, the amendment proposal failed in the Senate by two votes. Another year would pass before Congress would take up the matter again.

World War I ended on November 11, 1918, but the battle for woman's suffrage raged on in the United States. There were one hundred days left before the present Congress ended to work on securing the two votes needed to pass the amendment. If favorable action was not secured before March 4, 1919, the measure would have to be resubmitted again. Carrie Chapman Catt and the other leaders of the NAWSA began campaigns in the state that opposed woman's suffrage in hopes of winning over the necessary senators. Plans were also being made for a great demonstration at the Capitol in the middle of December to stir the members of the upper branch to favorable action. In addition to the campaigns launched, women from every state camped out in Washington, D.C. They formed a continuous, ever-present lobby in the Capitol building. There wasn't a senator or representative not subjected to the suffrage message.

Devoted women congregated in Lafayette Park to speak out about the Susan B. Anthony Suffrage Amendment. One of those women was a suffragist from El Paso, Texas, named Mrs. O. A. Critchett. "Men and women all over this land and others are watching and waiting to see what the Senate will do about the passage of the Susan B. Anthony Federal Amendment," she told the park audience. "Women all over the country are working with might and main to bring pressure to bear on the votes necessary in securing the two-thirds majority required for an affirmative vote.

"How any man now in the face of all that women have done during the last four years, and in particular during the time this country was at war, and all that women have done in the past, can hesitate for a moment in granting them what they should have had fifty years ago is a mystery.

"It can only be explained by saying that in free, democratic America, autocrats still live. In order to save our beloved country from criticism by foreign lands and people who do not understand our talk of democracy without its complete fulfillment, women should at once, now and always, have the right to a voice in the affairs of their own government."

All within earshot of Mrs. Critchett's words cheered and applauded. Their greatest hope was that at long last the day of triumph for the suffrage amendment was at hand.

In May 1919, both the United States House of Representatives and the Senate voted to approve the Susan B. Anthony Suffrage Amendment, also known as the Nineteenth Amendment. On June 4, 1919, Congress voted to pass the Nineteenth Amendment. One more hurdle remained. The bill needed to be ratified by the states.

The years spent establishing suffrage groups affiliated with the NAWSA would prove to be most beneficial at this point. In anticipation of this time, Carrie Chapman Catt had organized ratification committees in every state. Those committees were now called into action. They lobbied for suffrage with each state legislature. By September 1919, seventeen of the required thirty-one states had ratified the Nineteenth Amendment. On August 18, 1920, eleven months later, ratification was finally complete.

While waiting for the state legislatures to vote on the bill, Carrie founded a new organization called the League of Women Voters.

The near prospect of the suffrage amendment coming into being had prompted many women to ask, "What next? Shall we dissolve after the ratification of the amendment or is there a reason for continuance?" Carrie believed there should be a continuance. There was an appalling degree of inequality in women's status and unequal laws that still needed to be addressed. The league, with a chapter in every state, would be dedicated to teaching women about voting and politics. The league was to be nonpartisan and dedicated to always working on vital issues concerning to members and the public.

On August 26, 1920, at three-thirty in the afternoon, President Wilson welcomed Carrie Chapman Catt, Mrs. Helen Gardner, and members of the Civil Service Commission into his office to extend his congratulations on the suffrage victory. Secretary of State Bainbridge Colby offered his praise to the women as well. "I congratulate the women of the country upon the successful culmination of their efforts," Secretary Colby said, "which have been sustained in the face of many discouragements and which have now been finally realized."

Prominent suffragists from every state gathered in New York on Friday, August 27, 1920, to celebrate the formal ratification of the Nineteenth Amendment. "This is a glorious and wonderful day," Catt announced to the women. "Now that we have the vote, let us remember that we are no longer petitioners. We are not the wards of the nations but free and equal citizens."

Immediately after the Nineteenth Amendment was passed, chapters of then League of Women Voters across the nation went to work. Their slogan was "Every woman a voter in 1920." To bring about the end desired, an intensive campaign was launched to encourage all women to register to vote and to teach them the mechanics of voting. The enfranchisement of women in 1920 was the largest extension of suffrage ever made at one time by any organized and orderly government. Women everywhere eagerly undertook to see the extension of suffrage

Alice Paul displays the suffrage banner marked with stars for every state that ratified the Nineteenth Amendment. Library of Congress

intelligently carried into effect. The League had no interest in party affili-
ation selected by the woman voter. They merely urged and insisted that
all women get out and vote—join one party or another and do their full
duty as citizens.

"The league is well organized," the September 19, 1920, edition of
the *Evening Star* noted. "It inherited 3,500,000 members of the old suffrage associations located in all the states, counties, cities, and towns. The
national organization is headed by Mrs. Maud Wood Park of Boston,
and Carrie Chapman Catt is the honorary chairman. Then, the country
is divided into seven 'regions' each with a regional director. Next come
the state leagues, and then the county and city organizations. It is a most
compact and efficient organization and one that is showing results."

The fact that women could now vote and were being encouraged to
become a member of the League of Women Voters was not well received
by everyone. Many husbands struggled with the fact that their wives
could vote. In Nebraska, some of the husbands were objecting to their
spouses joining the organization and registering to vote. "This is going
to be a difficult adjustment period for some men," Mrs. A. J. Bowron,
chairman of the Nebraska League of Women Voters, wrote in a message
sent to the organization's headquarters. "I suspect there will be many
disagreements in households here. Some men have even told their wives
that if they vote, they will leave them."

On November 2, 1920, women went to the polls for the first time
since the passage of the Nineteenth Amendment. In Oregon, merchants
took full advantage of women being out that day by offering special dis-
counts for groceries and fabric to be purchased either before or after
they voted. In Idaho, women sang "My Country Tis of Thee" while
waiting in line to vote. "Those silent mounds across the sea where young
American men died in the war bid you carry out the purpose for which
they gave their lives," voter Joan Newburg told reporters at the *Idaho
State Journal*. "How could I not honor those men?" In Everett, Kansas,

one female voter recited a poem to the citizens who gathered to cast their ballots. "They said we wouldn't do it; they said we wouldn't do it," the poem began. "That lovely, lovely women would never have the cheek. Besides it would be inhuman for gentle, tender woman to cast a horrid ballot, and thus, as were to speak, her doubt of man's veracity, also of his capacity to govern and protect the imbeciles and the weak. That is the way the men, I say, talked of us women voting."

Seventy-two years had passed since suffragists began their struggle at the Seneca Falls Convention and the efforts of countless women, both celebrated and anonymous, guaranteed that woman's suffrage would become a reality.

The effort to fulfill the promise of the Declaration of Independence did not end with the vote. Voting was just the first step in the fight for equality. Just like the Founding Fathers, the women called suffragists were revolutionaries. They challenged the government and the country to change its view of the role of women in society. That view changed forever when women in mass first went to the polls in November 1920.

CHAPTER TEN

---•◦•---

Legacy: From Seneca Falls to the League of Women Voters

I go for all sharing the privileges of the government who assist in bearing its burdens, by no means excluding women.

—ABRAHAM LINCOLN,
SIXTEENTH PRESIDENT OF THE UNITED STATES

The watershed year of 1848, in the strife-filled period before the American Civil War, saw the rise of women at Seneca Falls who declared that they were equal to men and not just worthy of the vote—deserving of it by the divine right of being human and citizens. Of course, while that organized group was determined to fight for the equality of women, they were fighting at a time when the equality of all people was the central question of the day. The denial of rights to women and blacks (freed and slave) was incongruous with the enlightenment ideals of democracy and the hopes of a new republic—but those in charge of the new republic were having a tough time seeing past the blinders of their race and sex.

During and immediately after the Civil War, many abolitionists and suffragists worked together toward the common goal of ending slavery, and in 1866, after the end of the war, Elizabeth Cady Stanton and Susan B. Anthony formed the American Equal Rights Association intending to continue the fight for voting and civil rights for all citizens.

A pro-woman etching that updates the famous fresco Brumidi in the Rotunda of the Capital, *giving women their rightful place.* Library of Congress

That was when things got complicated.

As part of the process of reconstructing the Confederate states into the Union, Congress became absorbed in passing the Fourteenth and Fifteenth Amendments to the Constitution, amendments that defined both who qualified for citizenship regardless of race and sex and that drew criteria for who could vote in elections. The interpretation of the language in both amendments drew challenges from all sides—and ultimately split the previously strong movement in favor of suffrage for all former slaves and women into factions who were in favor of the political expedience of allowing males of African descent the right to vote regardless of their previous state of servitude while letting women's interest be pushed to the side.

But the split was more complicated than that. In the late 1860s, a further division erupted between women's suffrage advocates after the

National American Woman Suffrage Association. Library of Congress

Fourteenth and Fifteenth were the law of the land. The faction led by Elizabeth Cady Stanton and Susan B. Anthony favored taking swift action to enact national woman suffrage through yet another constitutional amendment. The faction led by Lucy Stone, Henry Blackwell, and Julia Ward Howe—once staunch allies of Stanton and Anthony in the struggle for suffrage and the end to slavery—favored using the clause of the Fifteenth that gave the states the right to decide who could vote. They wanted to approach the woman suffrage issue one state at a time.

After the Civil War, Anthony and Stanton launched a national effort to mobilize women to win suffrage for themselves. They began publishing a weekly newspaper, the *Revolution*, in 1868. They founded the National Woman Suffrage Association (NWSA) in 1869. Their style was confrontational. To demonstrate that no political party could take women for granted, they shocked their Republican allies by appealing for a woman suffrage plank to the Democratic National Convention in 1868. They explored alliances with labor unions, free-love advocates, Marxists, marriage reformers, and spiritualists. Their politics and their

The Rise of Women: The WCTU and other Reform Clubs

As waves of reform washed across the United States in the 1870s, women's groups—many newly energized by the success of woman abolitionists and the rise of woman suffrage organizations—prompted the creation of other women's groups and clubs bent on improving lives. The rationale for the disenfranchised women of America taking up causes for the less fortunate was straightforward. Women were civilizers. Their natural sphere—care for the home and family—made it natural that they would care about other women and their families. It was an inroad into political and social reform that some grabbed with both hands.

Founded in Ohio in 1874, the Woman's Christian Temperance Union (WCTU) is probably the most famous of the progressive women's organizations of the late nineteenth and early twentieth centuries. Under the leadership of Frances Willard, who took the helm of the organization in 1879, the WCTU became one of the biggest and most influential progressive reform groups in the country. The group actively campaigned for prison reform, labor laws, and woman suffrage throughout the end of the nineteenth century.

During the last two decades of the nineteenth century, volunteerism was on the rise among middle and upper class women who—thanks to greater economic and personal freedom— had time on their hands. These women became workers and activists for the progressive causes that seemed to flow naturally from their sphere of influence—civilizers and protectors of home and family. Local civic clubs and charities drew women together. Women's clubs and societies formed around common interests and then turned to causes like suffrage, temperance, and other social reforms. Organizations such as the Women's Trade Union League, the National Consumers League, and the WCTU were closely linked with suffrage, and particularly the National American Woman Suffrage Association by 1890.

A main focus of the WCTU was always temperance—which to them meant the prohibition of the sale and consumption of alcohol. Through the work of more than a thousand local branches of the organization and the publication of a journal called *Our Union* the WCTU effectively lobbied for local-option Prohibition and made inroads on their other issues—including suffrage. The WCTU was equally effective as a partner for suffrage and a detractor. As an organization, their means of lobbying was effective. But their partnership gave pro-alcohol groups a reason to oppose suffrage. At the start of the twentieth century, however, the group distanced itself from the vote in favor of their primary goal—eventually affecting the passage of the Eighteenth Amendment in 1919. The WCTU would remain an organization through much of the twentieth century, even after Prohibition was repealed.

alliances contributed to the formation late in 1869 of the rival, respectable, and soundly Republican American Woman Suffrage Association, led by Lucy Stone.

The national association focused on national suffrage, in the belief that states did not have the constitutional power to deprive American citizens of their right to vote. After 1876, the NWSA pushed hard for passage of a sixteenth constitutional amendment that would prohibit disfranchisement on account of sex. With its eye on Congress, the NWSA met annually in Washington, D.C. where Susan B. Anthony and her coworkers became proficient and familiar lobbyists.

Anthony's strength in the 1880s was to build bridges between suffragists and the burgeoning woman's movement. She courted the Woman's Christian Temperance Union, oversaw the founding of the International and National Councils of Women, and pursued the merger in 1890 of the national and American associations into the National American Woman Suffrage Association (NAWSA). The expanding movement called for strong leadership. Anthony mediated differences over cooperating with Mormon women, clashes between white Southerners and Northern blacks, and collisions between secularists and evangelical Christians. She also tried to keep the NAWSA focused on winning suffrage from the federal government rather than from each state.

Anthony was eighty years old when she retired from the presidency of the NAWSA. She nonetheless crossed the United States one more time by train to lend support to western suffragists, and she attended her last national suffrage meeting one month before her death. She died at home in Rochester in March 1906.

This book tells the story of the fight for suffrage with a focus on the efforts that, on a state-by-state basis shaped the spread of suffrage across the western United States in the years leading up to the ratification of the Nineteenth Amendment—an effort that took millions of woman hours over more than half a century and of the larger fight for women's rights

Members of the national council of the women's party lay a wreath in honor of Susan B. Anthony's birthday. Library of Congress

that occupied the nation in the nineteenth and twentieth centuries. The reasons for the early success of the efforts to gain the vote in the West are as varied as the states and the women who lobbied for their rights, but it's important to note that they also happened in concert with the major national movement. Each effort likely would not have succeeded without the other.

In the hundred years since Tennessee ratified the Nineteenth Amendment, formalizing American women's place as equal voting citizens under the Constitution of the United States, the fight for the franchise has not ended. Throughout the twentieth century, restrictions on Native American voting rights, Jim Crow laws in the South, and other forms of intimidation kept citizens from the polls. In the twenty-first century, other tactics continue to be used to restrict the rights of voters, and voter turnout, even in the most contentious of elections, averages around 60 percent. Yet, when seen from the long view of history, the path from Mary Wollstonecraft to Elizabeth Cady Stanton to Abigail Scott Duniway to Jeannette Rankin to the ratification of the Susan B. Anthony Amendment looks like an inevitable march across the country toward an inevitable result. And it is too easy to imagine the scene in sepia tones populated by men and women in quaint old-fashioned dress and to dismiss the real fears of women denied property, the custody of children, and a political voice—just because of their sex. As the beneficiaries of their efforts, we should not ignore the sacrifices and radical adjustment of thinking that were the required elements of success.

Woman Suffrage Organizations

The National American Woman Suffrage Association

The NAWSA emerged in 1890 when the National Woman Suffrage Association, led by Elizabeth Cady Stanton and Susan B. Anthony, and the American Woman Suffrage Association, led by Lucy Stone, Henry Blackwell, and Julia Ward Howe—set aside their differences and joined forces. Since the 1860s, the NWSA favored women's enfranchisement through a federal constitutional amendment, while AWSA believed success could be more easily achieved through state-by-state campaigns. NAWSA combined both of these techniques, securing the passage of the Nineteenth Amendment in 1920 through a series of well-orchestrated state campaigns under the dynamic direction of Carrie Chapman Catt. Once NAWSA's primary goal of women's enfranchisement was a reality, the organization was transformed into the League of Women Voters.

The Alpha Suffrage Club

The Alpha Suffrage Club was an organization of African American women who studied political and civic questions that affected African American women across the nation. They participated in numerous suffrage parades.

American Equal Rights Association

Founded in 1866, the organization worked to secure equal rights, especially the right of suffrage, for all American citizens.

American Woman Suffrage Association

The AWSA was formed in 1869 in response to a split in the American Equal Rights Association over the Fifteenth

Amendment to the United States Constitution. Its founders were staunch abolitionists who strongly supported securing the right to vote for African American men. They believed that the Fifteenth Amendment would be in danger of failing to pass in Congress if it included the vote for women. On the other side of the split in the American Equal Rights Association, opposing the Fifteenth Amendment, were Elizabeth Cady Stanton and Susan B. Anthony.

College Equal Suffrage League

The College Equal Suffrage League was an American woman suffrage organization founded in 1900 by Maud Wood Park and Inez Haynes Irwin as a way to attract younger Americans to the women's rights movement. The league spurred the creation of college branches around the country and influenced the actions of other prominent groups such as the National American Woman Suffrage Association.

The Congressional Union for Woman Suffrage

After 1900, some younger members of the National Woman Suffrage Association, the organization that formed to reconcile the rift that had occurred in the movement during Reconstruction, became impatient about the progress the national organization was making in pursuit of the franchise for all American women. While studying at the School of Economics and Political Science in London, a young American named Alice Paul joined the militant Women's Social and Political Union. Her time with that more militant organization caused her to be arrested and imprisoned three times with other leaders in the movement, even going on hunger strikes and being force-fed. Back in the United States, Paul would form the Congressional Union for Woman Suffrage and use some of the tactics of her British sisters to forward the goals of suffrage.

National Woman's Party

The National Woman's Party grew out of the Congressional Union for Woman Suffrage, becoming a fully fledged American political party that in the early part of the twentieth century employed militant methods to fight for an equal rights amendment to the U.S. Constitution. The organization was headed by Alice Paul and Lucy Burns.

The Silent Sentinels

Organized by Alice Paul, Lucy Burns, and the National Woman's Party, this group of women protested in front of the White House and demanded woman suffrage. The women began on January 10, 1917, and protested for six days a week until June 4, 1919, when the Nineteenth Amendment to the United States Constitution was passed both by the House of Representatives and the Senate.

Women's groups gather to celebrate the installation of the sculpture portrait of three suffragists at the U.S. Capitol, circa 1923. Library of Congress

Equal Franchise Party

The Equal Franchise Party was a state-by-state organization that advocated woman suffrage in the United States. Created and joined by women of wealth, it was a conduit through which the energies of upper-class women could be channeled into political activism conducted within a socially comfortable environment.

Women's Trade Union League

Founded in 1903, the group's focus was on assisting the wage-earning women of the United States to win the right to vote and to work toward gaining equal pay and fairer conditions in all areas of employment.

BIBLIOGRAPHY

———•●•———

Books

Babcock, Barbara. *Woman Lawyer: The Trials of Clara Foltz*. Palo Alto, CA: Stanford University Press, 2012.

Baker, Jean H. *Sisters: The Lives of America's Suffragists*. New York: Hill & Wang, 2006.

———. *Votes for Women: The Struggle for Suffrage Revisited*. London: Oxford University Press, 2002.

Block, Judy Rachel. *The First Woman in Congress: Jeannette Rankin*. New York: C.P.I., 1978.

Buhle, Mari Jo, and Paul Buhle. *The Concise History of Woman Suffrage*. Champaign: University of Illinois Press, 1978.

Clark, Rebekah Ryan. "An Uncovered History: Mormons in the Woman Suffrage Movement, 1896–1920." *In New Scholarship on Latter-day Saint Women in the Twentieth Century: Selections from the Women's History Initiative Seminars, 2003–2004*, edited by Carol Cornwall Madsen and Cherry B. Silver. Provo, UT: Joseph Fielding Smith Institute for LDS History, 2005.

Davidson, Sue. *A Heart in Politics: Jeannette Rankin and Patsy T. Mink*. Seattle, WA: Seal Press, 1994.

Dubois, Ellen C. *Harriot Stanton Blanton: Winning of Woman Suffrage*. New Haven, CT: Yale University Press, 1997.

———. *Woman's Suffrage and Women's Rights*. New York: New York University Press, 1947.

Duniway, Abigail Scott. *Path Breaking: An Autobiographical History of the Equal Suffrage Movement in the Pacific Coast States*. Portland, OR: James, Kerns & Abbott, 1914.

Enss, Chris. *Hearts West: Mail Order Brides on the Western Frontier*. Guilford, CT: TwoDot Books, 2005.

———. *Tales behind the Tombstones: The Deaths and Burials of the Old West's Most Nefarious Outlaws, Notorious Women, and Celebrated Lawmen.* Guilford, CT: TwoDot Books, 2007.

Evans, Sarah M. *Born for Liberty: A History of Women in America.* New York: Free Press, 1989.

Faragher, John. *Women and Men on the Overland Trail.* Rev. ed. New Haven, CT: Yale University Press, 2001.

Faulkner, Carol. *Lucretia Mott's Heresy: Abolition and Women's Rights in Nineteenth-Century America.* Philadelphia: University of Pennsylvania Press, 2011.

Flexner, Eleanor. *Century of Struggle: The Woman's Rights Movement in the United States.* Cambridge, MA: Belknap Press, 1996

Gaughen, Shasta. *Why Women Should Vote: Women's Rights.* San Diego, CA: Greenhaven, 2003.

———. *Women Have No Need to Vote: Women's Rights.* San Diego, CA: Greenhaven, 2003.

Gavin, Lettie. *American Women in World War I: They Also Served.* Boulder: University Press of Colorado, 1997.

Giles, Kevin S. *Flight of the Dove: The Story of Jeannette Rankin.* Beaverton, OR: Touchstone Press, 1980.

Griffith, Elisabeth. *In Her Own Right: The Life of Elizabeth Cady Stanton.* London: Oxford University Press, 1985.

Gullett, Gayle. *Becoming Citizens: The Emergence and Development of the California Women's Movement, 1880–1911.* Chicago: University of Illinois Press, 2000.

Hankins, Barry. *The Second Great Awakening and the Transcendentalists.* Westport, CT: Greenwood Press, 2004.

Harper, Ida Husted. *The Life and Work of Susan B. Anthony including Public Addresses, Her Own Letters and Many from Her Contemporaries during Fifty Years.* Vol. 1 of 2. Indianapolis, IN: Bowen-Merrill, 1898.

Hinks, Peter P, John R. McKivigan, and R. Owen Williams. *Encyclopedia of Antislavery and Abolition: Greenwood Milestones in African American History.* Westport, CT: Greenwood Press, 2007.

Isenberg, Nancy. *Sex and Citizenship in Antebellum America.* Chapel Hill: University of North Carolina Press, 1998.

Josephson, Hannah Geffen. *Jeannette Rankin, First Lady in Congress: A Biography.* Indianapolis, IN: Bobbs-Merrill, 1974.

Kerr, Andrea Moore. *Lucy Stone: Speaking Out for Equality*. New Brunswick, NJ: Rutgers University Press, 1992.

Kraditor, Aileen. *The Ideas of the Woman Suffrage Movement 1890–1920*. New York: W. W. Norton, 1981.

Larson, T. A. *History of Wyoming*. Lincoln: University of Nebraska Press, 1965.

Lerner, Gerda, and Sarah Moore Grimké. *The Feminist Thought of Sarah Grimké*. New York: Oxford University Press, 1998.

Lopach, James J., and Jean A. Luckowski. *Jeannette Rankin: A Political Woman*. Boulder: University Press of Colorado, 2005.

Lutz, Alma. *Susan B. Anthony: Rebel, Crusader, Humanitarian*. Portland, OR: CreateSpace, 2014.

Madsen, Carol Cornwall. *An Advocate for Women: The Public Life of Emmeline B. Wells, 1870–1920*. Provo, UT: Brigham Young University Press, 2006.

———. *Battle for the Ballot: Essays on Woman Suffrage in Utah, 1870–1896*. Provo, UT: Brigham Young University Press, 1997.

Mani, Bonnie G. *Women, Power, and Political Change*. Lanham, MD: Lexington Books, 2007.

May, Martha. *Women's Roles in Twentieth-Century America*. Westport, CT: Greenwood Press, 2009.

McMillen, Sally Gregory. *Seneca Falls and the Origins of the Women's Rights Movement*. London: Oxford University Press, 2008.

Mead, Rebecca J. *How the Vote Was Won: Woman Suffrage in the Western United States, 1868–1914*. New York: New York University Press, 2004.

Morrison, Dorothy N. *Ladies Were Not Expected: Abigail Scott Duniway and Women's Rights*. New York: Atheneum Books, 1977.

Newman, Vivien. *We Also Served: The Forgotten Women of the First World War*. Barnsley, UK: Pen & Sword Books, 2014.

Powers, Roger S. *Protest, Power, and Change: An Encyclopedia of Nonviolent Action from ACT-UP to Women's Suffrage*. New York: Routledge, 1997.

Saldin, Robert P. *War, the American State, and Politics since 1898*. Cambridge: Cambridge University Press, 2010.

Smith, Bonnie G. *The Oxford Encyclopedia of Women in World History*. London: Oxford University Press, 2008.

Smith, Norma. *Jeannette Rankin: America's Conscience*. Helena: Montana Historical Society Press, 2002.

Somervill, Barbara A. *Votes for Women! The Story of Carrie Chapman Catt*. Greensboro, NC: Morgan Reynolds, 2003.

Stalcup, Brenda. *Women's Suffrage*. Turning Points in World History. San Diego, CA: Greenhaven, 2000.

Stanton, Elizabeth Cady. *A Brief Biography of Susan B. Anthony*. Brighton, MI: Cornell Publications, 1905.

——. *Eighty Years and More*. Boston: Northeastern University Press, 1993.

Stevenson, Shanna. *Women's Votes, Women's Voices: The Campaign for Equal Rights in Washington*. Tacoma: Washington State University Press, 2009.

Tetrault, Lisa. *The Myth of Seneca Falls: Memory and the Women's Suffrage Movement, 1848–1898*. Chapel Hill: University of North Carolina Press, 2014.

Ulrich, Laurel Thatcher. *Well-Behaved Women Seldom Make History*. New York: Alfred Knopf, 2007.

Van Wagenen, Lola. *Sister-Wives and Suffragists: Polygamy and the Politics of Woman Suffrage 1870–1896*. Provo, UT: Brigham Young University Studies, 2012.

Wellman, Judith. *The Road to Seneca Falls: Elizabeth Cady Stanton and the First Women's Rights Convention*. Champaign: University of Illinois Press, 2004.

White, Florence Meiman. *First Woman in Congress: Jeannette Rankin*. New York: J. Messner, 1980.

White, Jean Bickmore. "Women's Suffrage in Utah." In *Utah History Encyclopedia*, edited by Allen Kent Powell. Salt Lake City: University of Utah Press, 1994.

Wolbrecht, Christina. *The Politics of Women's Rights Parties, Positions, and Change*. Princeton, NJ: Princeton University Press, 2000.

Magazines, Journals, and Other Sources

Alexander, Thomas G. "An Experiment in Progressive Legislation: The Granting of Woman Suffrage in Utah in 1870." *Utah Historical Quarterly* 38 (Winter 1970).

Alonso, Harriet Hyman. "Jeannette Rankin and the Women's Peace Union." *Montana: The Magazine of Western History* 39 (Spring 1989): 34–49.

——. "'To Make War Legally Impossible': A Study of the Women's Peace Union, 1921–1942." PhD diss., State University of New York at Stony Brook, 1986.

Amaro, Charlotte A. "Across Contexts and through Time: Jeannette Rankin, Feminine Style, and an Ethic of Care." PhD diss., Wayne State University, 2000.

Arizona State Library. Archives and Public Records, SG 10 Women's Suffrage, box 1, folder 1.

Beeton, Beverly. "Woman Suffrage in Territorial Utah." *Utah Historical Quarterly* 46 (1986).

Board, John C. "Jeannette Rankin: The Lady from Montana." *Montana: The Magazine of Western History* 17 (July 1967): 2–17.

———. "The Lady from Montana: Jeannette Rankin." Master's thesis, University of Wyoming, 1964.

Bonner, Helen Louise Ward. "The Jeannette Rankin Story." PhD diss., Ohio University, 1982.

California Legislature, Thirtieth and Thirty-Ninth Sessions (1911). Transcript.

Cooper, Donald G. "The California Suffrage Campaign of 1896: Its Origin, Strategies, Defeat." *Southern California Quarterly* 17, no. 4 (Winter 1989).

Ewig, Rick. "Did She Do That? Examining Ester Morris' Role in the Passage of the Suffrage Act." *Annals of Wyoming* 78, no. 1 (Winter 2006).

Fleming, Sidney Howell. "Solving the Jigsaw Puzzle: One Suffrage Story at a Time." *Annals of Wyoming* 62, no. 1 (Spring 1990).

Hardaway, Roger D. "Jeannette Rankin: The Early Years." *North Dakota Quarterly* 48 (Winter 1980): 62–68.

Harper's Bazaar, May 26, 1900.

Harris, Ted Carlton. "Jeannette Rankin: Suffragist, First Woman Elected to Congress, and Pacifist." PhD diss., University of Georgia, 1972.

———. "Jeannette Rankin, Warring Pacifist." Master's thesis, University of Georgia, 1969.

"Jeannette Rankin" in *Women in Congress, 1917–2006*. Prepared under the direction of the Committee on House Administration by the Office of History and Preservation, U.S. House of Representatives, Government Printing Office, Washington, DC, 2006.

Jones, Nancy Baker. "A Forgotten Feminist: The Early Writing of Ida Husted Harper, 1878–1894." *Indiana Magazine of History* 73, no. 2 (June 1977).

Journal of Mormon History 17 (1991). University of Illinois Press.

Larson, T. A. "Petticoats at the Polls: Woman Suffrage in Territorial Wyoming." *Pacific Northwest Quarterly* 44, no. 2 (1953).

———. "Woman Suffrage in Western America." *Utah Historical Quarterly* 38, no. 1 (Winter 1970).

Massie, Michael A. "Reform Is Where You Find It: The Roots of Woman Suffrage in Wyoming." *Annals of Wyoming* 62, no. 1 (Spring 1990).

Miller, Grant. "Women's Suffrage, Political Responsiveness, and Child Survival in American History." *Quarterly Journal of Economics* 123, no. 3 (2008).

National Police Gazette, April 22, 1882.

Nevada County Historical Archives. Letters between Susan B. Anthony, Ellen Sargent, and Aaron Sargent, 1871–1911.

Nevada County Historical Archives. Journals kept by Ellen Sargent and Aaron Sargent, 1871–1911.

Pioneers Magazine, Nevada City, California, August 9, 1978, and October 25, 1978.

Relief Society Handbook. "Administering the Church." Church of Latter Day Saints, 2010.

Schaffer, Ronald. "Jeannette Rankin, Progressive Isolationist." PhD diss., Princeton University, 1959.

Stansell, Christine. "The Road from Seneca Falls." *New Republic* 219, no. 6 (1998): 26–38.

Welter, Barbara. "The Cult of True Womanhood, 1820–1860." *American Quarterly* 16 (1996).

White, Jean Bickmore. "Woman's Place Is in the Constitution: The Struggle for Equal Rights in Utah in 1895." *Utah Historical Quarterly 42, no. 4: 344–69.*

Wilson, Joan Hoff. "'Peace Is a Woman's Job . . .': Jeannette Rankin and American Foreign Policy: Her Lifework as a Pacifist." *Montana: The Magazine of Western History* 30 (January 1980): 29–41; (April 1980): 38–53.

Young, Louise. "Women's Place in American Politics: The Historical Perspective." *Journal of Politics* (1976).

Newspapers

Anti-Slavery Bugle Lisbon, Ohio, June 21, 1851

Austin American Austin, Texas, August 22, 1920

Baltimore Sun Baltimore, Maryland, August 24, 1913

Billings Weekly Gazette Billings, Montana, February 11, 1898

Boston Globe Boston, Massachusetts, October 19, 1893

Boston Globe Boston, Massachusetts, April 26, 1900

Boston Globe Boston, Massachusetts, September 3, 1916

Broad Ax Salt Lake City, Utah, November 15, 1913

Brooklyn Daily Eagle Brooklyn, New York, May 1, 1910

Brooklyn Eagle Brooklyn, New York, February 15, 1870

Buffalo Enquirer Buffalo, New York, August 24, 1920

Caldwell Tribune Caldwell, Idaho, February 20, 1897

Capital Journal Salem, Oregon, October 11, 1915

Casper Star-Tribune Casper, Wyoming, December 26, 1963

Charlotte News Charlotte, North Carolina, August 25, 1918

Chattanooga News Chattanooga, Tennessee, August 26, 1920

Cheyenne Leader Cheyenne, Wyoming, April 28, 1870

Chicago Tribune Chicago, Illinois, November 12, 1863

Chicago Tribune Chicago, Illinois, June 2, 1880

Chicago Tribune Chicago, Illinois, March 25, 1888

Chicago Tribune Chicago, Illinois, December 28, 1900

Clarion-Ledger Jackson, Mississippi, April 28, 1940

Colfax Gazette Colfax, Washington, February 26, 1909

Commoner Lincoln, Nebraska, August 1, 1913

Courier-Journal Louisville, Kentucky, April 29, 1900

Daily Herald Provo, Utah, April 8, 1976

Daily Kansas Tribune Lawrence, Kansas, May 3, 1872

Daily Milwaukee News Milwaukee, Wisconsin, November 14, 1866

Daily Signal Crowley, Louisiana, January 11, 1918

Daily Times Davenport, Iowa, May 25, 1916

Decatur Herald Decatur, Illinois, November 2, 1920

Democrat and Chronicle Rochester, New York, March 19, 1931

Desert Evening News Salt Lake City, Utah, April 12, 1888

Desert News Salt Lake City, Utah, April 25, 1888

Desert News Weekly San Bernardino, California, February 10, 1869

East Oregonian Pendleton, Oregon, June 29, 1905

Elmore Bulletin Rocky Bar, Idaho, September 30, 1896

El Paso Herald El Paso, Texas, December 21, 1918

Emporia Gazette Emporia, Kansas, March 13, 1906

Evening Dispatch Provo, Utah, March 30, 1895

Evening Star Washington, D.C., February 20, 1895

Evening Star Washington, D.C., July 14, 1917

Evening Star Washington, D.C., September 19, 1920

Grand Forks Herald Grand Forks, North Dakota, September 6, 1916

Great Falls Tribune Great Falls, Montana, August 3, 1916

Great Falls Tribune Great Falls, Montana, May 10, 1918

Great Falls Tribune Great Falls, Montana, September 4, 1927

Greenville Journal Greenville, Ohio, January 17, 1918

Harrisburg Telegraph Harrisburg, Pennsylvania, January 29, 1870

Hartford Courant Hartford, Connecticut, September 20, 1946

Idaho State Journal Pocatello, Idaho, November 4, 1920

Idaho Statesman Boise, Idaho, December 8, 1898

Indiana State Journal Indianapolis, Indiana, March 29, 1882

Inter Ocean Chicago, Illinois, April 13, 1884

Lawrence Daily World Lawrence, Kansas, November 10, 1896

Lead Daily Call Lead, South Dakota, January 1, 1914

Leavenworth Times Leavenworth, Kansas, November 26, 1869

Leavenworth Weekly Times Leavenworth, Kansas, July 14, 1881

Lewiston Daily Teller Lewiston, Idaho, August 15, 1889

Lewiston Daily Teller Lewiston, Idaho, December 24, 1896

Los Angeles Herald Los Angeles, California, September 21, 1875

Los Angeles Times Los Angeles, California, September 14, 1882

Los Angeles Times Los Angeles, California, April 12, 1896

Los Angeles Times Los Angeles, California, June 13, 1896

Los Angeles Times Los Angeles, California, February 19, 1902

Los Angeles Times Los Angeles, California, October 1, 1911

Los Angeles Times Los Angeles, California, June 8, 1916

Los Angeles Times Los Angeles, California, March 25, 1917

Los Angeles Times Los Angeles, California, August 28, 1920

Marion Star Marion, Ohio, November 11, 1898

Marysville Journal-Tribune Marysville, Ohio, May 14, 1917

Montgomery Advertiser Montgomery, Alabama, July 27, 1913

Morning Astoria Astoria, Oregon, March 10, 1881

National Republican Washington, D.C., October 21, 1881

New Northwest Portland, Oregon, April 26, 1872

New Northwest Portland, Oregon, November 28, 1873

New Northwest Portland, Oregon, July 14, 1876

New Northwest Portland, Oregon, April 19, 1878

News-Press Fort Myers, Florida, February 7, 1993

New York Times New York, New York, February 14, 1870

New York Times New York, New York, January 7, 1911

New York Tribune New York, New York, July 27, 1913

Northwest Herald Woodstock, Illinois, February 7, 1993

Oakland Tribune Oakland, California, September 28, 1882

Oakland Tribune Oakland, California, August 15, 1887

Oakland Tribune Oakland, California, March 7, 1909

Oakland Tribune Oakland, California, July 26, 1911

Oregon Argus Oregon City, Oregon, October 19, 1859

Oregon Argus Oregon City, Oregon, October 24, 1859

Oregon Argus Oregon City, Oregon, November 2, 1859

Oregon Daily Journal Portland, Oregon, February 2, 1917

Oregon Daily Journal Portland, Oregon, September 14, 1918

Ottawa Daily Republic Ottawa, Kansas, June 3, 1901

Petaluma Daily Morning Courier Petaluma, California, November 21, 1910

Petaluma Weekly Argus Petaluma, California, July 7, 1882

Pittsburgh Daily Post Pittsburgh, Pennsylvania, September 9, 1916

Pittsburgh Post-Gazette Pittsburgh, Pennsylvania, May 10, 1915

Record-Union Sacramento, California, January 3, 1896

Red Cloud Chief Red Cloud, Nebraska, May 14, 1897

Rochester Herald Rochester, New York, July 18, 1895

Sacramento Daily Union Sacramento, California, May 29, 1896

Saint Paul Globe St. Paul, Minnesota, November 24, 1882

Salt Lake Herald Salt Lake City, Utah, April 7, 1881

Salt Lake Herald Salt Lake City, Utah, May 31, 1882

Salt Lake Herald Salt Lake City, Utah, June 18, 1882

Salt Lake Herald Salt Lake City, Utah, March 26, 1886

Salt Lake Herald Salt Lake City, Utah, February 10, 1889

Salt Lake Herald Salt Lake City, Utah, April 12, 1889

Salt Lake Herald Salt Lake City, Utah, October 13, 1889

Salt Lake Herald Salt Lake City, Utah, March 7, 1890

Salt Lake Herald Salt Lake City, Utah, March 30, 1890

Salt Lake Herald Salt Lake City, Utah, March 31, 1895

Salt Lake Herald Salt Lake City, Utah, April 4, 1895

Salt Lake Herald Salt Lake City, Utah, April 5, 1895

Salt Lake Herald Salt Lake City, Utah, April 6, 1895

Salt Lake Herald Salt Lake City, Utah, April 7, 1895

Salt Lake Herald Salt Lake City, Utah, April 16, 1895

Salt Lake Herald Salt Lake City, Utah, April 19, 1895

Salt Lake Herald Salt Lake City, Utah, April 28, 1895

Salt Lake Herald Salt Lake City, Utah, April 30, 1895

Salt Lake Herald Salt Lake City, Utah, May 13, 1895

Salt Lake Herald Salt Lake City, Utah, December 2, 1898

Salt Lake Herald Salt Lake City, Utah, March 20, 1918

Salt Lake Tribune Salt Lake City, Utah, August 14, 1919

San Bernardino News San Bernardino, California, February 6, 1918

San Francisco Call San Francisco, California, March 17, 1896

San Francisco Call San Francisco, California, May 3, 1896

San Francisco Call San Francisco, California, July 4, 1909

San Francisco Call San Francisco, California, July 26, 1911

San Francisco Call San Francisco, California, October 9, 1911

San Francisco Call San Francisco, California, October 14, 1911

San Francisco Call San Francisco, California, October 20, 1911

San Francisco Chronicle San Francisco, California, January 29, 1878

San Francisco Chronicle San Francisco, California, March 24, 1896

San Francisco Chronicle San Francisco, California, November 7, 1917

Santa Ana Register Santa Ana, California, September 10, 1917

Santa Cruz Weekly Sentinel Santa Cruz, California, April 27, 1878

Seattle Post-Intelligencer Seattle, Washington, July 23, 1878

Seattle Post-Intelligencer Seattle, Washington, August 31, 1878

Seattle Post-Intelligencer Seattle, Washington, November 21, 1883

Seattle Post-Intelligencer Seattle, Washington, November 21, 1884

Seattle Post-Intelligencer Seattle, Washington, August 15, 1888

Seattle Times Seattle, Washington, March 5, 1909

Sheboygan Press Sheboygan, Wisconsin, January 10, 1918

Star Gazette Elmira, New York, July 16, 1998

Star Press Muncie, Indiana, March 16, 1931

Star-Tribune Minneapolis, Minnesota, December 12, 1999

Statesman Journal Salem, Oregon, January 24, 1904

Statesman Journal Salem, Oregon, November 6, 1971

Statesman Journal Salem, Oregon, June 6, 1976

Stevens Point Journal Stevens Point, Wisconsin, October 27, 1902

St. Helens Mist St. Helens, Oregon, October 15, 1915

Tacoma Times Tacoma, Washington, January 23, 1909

Times London, England, May 29, 1896

Times Shreveport, Louisiana, January 29, 1911

Times-Democrat New Orleans, Louisiana, March 21, 1903

Topeka Daily Capital Topeka, Kansas, September 16, 1917

Ukiah Dispatch Democrat Ukiah, California, September 8, 1911
Union Grass Valley, California, October 25, 1978
Utopian Beaver, Utah, January 20, 1891
Washington Herald Washington, D.C., November 18, 1918
Washington Post Washington, D.C., July 13, 1910
Washington Post Washington, D.C., September 5. 1920
Washington Standard Olympia, Washington, November 4, 1871
Waterville Telegraph Waterville, Kansas, October 3, 1924
Wichita Eagle Wichita, Kansas, June 1, 1919
Woman's Exponent Salt Lake City, Utah, November 15, 1875
Woman's Exponent Salt Lake City, Utah, May 1, 1892
Woman's Exponent Salt Lake City, Utah, April 1, 1894
Wood River Times Hailey, Idaho, November 21, 1890

Websites

www.archives.gov/historical-docs/todays-doc/index.html?dod-date=1112
www.biography.com/people/lucy-burns-063016
http://blogs.dickinson.edu/hist-211pinsker/2010/10/12/war-women-and-the-west
http://carlanthonyonline.com/2013/09/01/the-scruffy-dudes-who-got-Wyoming-women-the-vote
https://digitalcommons.usu.edu/cgi/viewcontent.cgi?article=1108&context=usupress_pubs
www.fairmormon.org/wpcontent/uploads/2017/03/MormonWomenProtest.pdf
www.futurity.org/mens-league-for-womens-suffrage
http://history.house.gov/Blog/2018/January/1-10-Suffrage-Committee
https://historylink.org/File/8566
https://historytogo.utah.gov/utah_chapters/statehood_and_the_progressive_era/struggleforstatehoodchronology.html
www.lds.org/handbook/handbook-2-administering-the-church/relief-society/lang=eng
https://millercenter.org/the-presidency/presidential-speeches/september-9-1916-message-regarding-womens-suffrage
www.nationalarchives.gov.uk/pathways/firstworldwar/document
www.nps.gov/articles/womens-suffrage-wwi.htm
https://oregonencyclopedia.org
www.pbs.org/stantonanthony/resources/abolitionists.html

www.senate.gov/artandhistory/history/minute/Senate-Passes-Woman
-Suffrage

www.theodoreroosevelt.org/site/c.elKSIdOWIiJ8H/b.9297493/k.7CB9
/Quotations_from_the_speeches_and_other_works_of
_Theodore_Roosevelt.htm

www.uen.org/utah_history_encyclopedia/g/GODBEITES.shtml

www.washingtonhistory.org/research/whc/milestones/aftersuffrage
/minutewomen

www.wyohistory.org/essays/right-choice-wrong-reasons-wyoming-women
-win-right-to-vote

INDEX

Italicized page numbers indicate illustrations. Maps are indicated with *m* following the page number.

ABOUT THE AUTHOR

Chris Enss is a *New York Times* best-selling author who has been writing about women of the Old West for more than twenty years. She has penned more than forty published books on the subject. Her book entitled *Entertaining Women: Actresses, Dancers, and Singers in the Old West* was a Spur Award finalist in 2017. Enss's book *Mochi's War: The Tragedy of Sand Creek* received the Will Rogers Medallion Award for Best Nonfiction Western for 2015. Her book entitled *Object Matrimony: The Risky Business of Mail-Order Matchmaking on the Western Frontier* won the Elmer Kelton Award for Best Nonfiction Book of 2013. Enss's book *Sam Sixkiller: Cherokee Frontier Lawman* was named Outstanding Book on Oklahoma History by the Oklahoma Historical Society.